1001 IDEAS FOR
COLOR
&PAINT

1001 IDEAS FOR
COLOR & PAINT

EMMA CALLERY

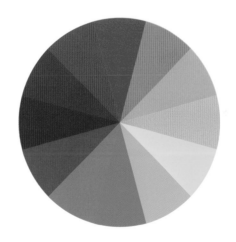

CREATIVE
HOMEOWNER®

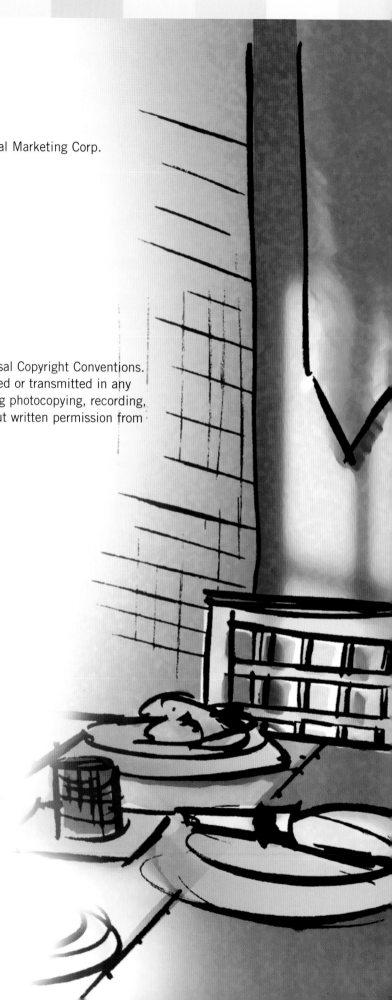

Copyright © 2006 Marshall Editions
All rights reserved

A Marshall Edition
Conceived, edited, and designed by Marshall Editions
The Old Brewery
6 Blundell Street
London N7 9BH
U.K.
www.quarto.com

ISBN-10: 1-58011-288-9
ISBN-13: 978-1-58011-288-8
Library of Congress Control Number: 2005931073

Current printing (last digit)
10 9 8 7 6 5 4 3 2

Originated in Hong Kong by Modern Age
Printed and bound in China

Publisher: Richard Green
Commissioning Editor: Claudia Martin
Art Direction: Ivo Marloh
Design: Alchemedia
Editor: Sharon Hynes
Illustrations: Ivo Marloh
Indexer: Jean Clarke
Production: Nikki Ingram

CREATIVE HOMEOWNER
A Division of Federal Marketing Corp.
24 Park Way
Upper Saddle River, NJ 07458

www.creativehomeowner.com

Contents

Introduction: Using Color and Paint   6

Choosing Color   14

     Naturals and Neutrals   16

     Pretty Pastels   32

     Warm and Cozy   48

     Hot Housing   64

     Mediterranean Magic   80

     Exotic Looks   94

     Contemporary Living   112

     Period Colors   132

     Enhancing Your Space   155

Choosing Paint Techniques   174

     Making Pictures   176

     Textural Finishes   192

     Faux Techniques   208

Practical Checklist   226

Glossary   232

Resource Guide   233

Index   236

Introduction: Using Color and Paint

If you want to dramatically transform the look of your home, the quickest and most cost-effective way is with paint. However, the huge choice of colors and painted effects may leave you agonizing over the simplest decisions. Before you play it safe, take a look at all of your options, as presented in *1001 Ideas for Color and Paint.*

This book provides practical guidance on how colors are perceived, what color schemes work (because there is no such thing as a bad color: just bad combinations), and how to achieve them. It starts with a set of chapters, each one exploring a different kind of color (for example, pastel colors or Mediterranean shades), showing how these palettes work together and with harmonizing and contrasting colors. These chapters also show room sets decorated in different color schemes so that you can judge their impact and understand how color sets the tone in the home.

There follows a comprehensive guide to choosing paint effects and mixing and matching effects with colors and soft furnishings. There is also practical advice on whether to undertake the effect yourself or to employ a professional. A "Practical Checklist" completes the book with all the factual information about the paints, materials, and professionals you could need. Before going further, it is worth getting some background on the topic of color.

UNDERSTANDING COLOR

Picture a rainbow. Do you see strips of pure colors, or bands that merge into one another so you can't see where each new hue begins? Rainbows are a good starting place for discussing color because they show the color spectrum of primary hues and reveal how the brain responds to these colors. The human eye sees rainbows as separate bands of color, when in reality each hue

Opposite: This kitchen mixes cool harmonizing hues of aqua and cream, which create a light and airy effect. The contrasting colors of russet and gold in the soft furnishings bring the scheme to life.
Above: In this simple monochromatic scheme of lilac and cream, interest is provided by tonal variation—between the mid-tone of the chairs and the pale light-reflecting walls.

blends with its neighbor. In the same way, note how boxes of the same size will look different sizes to us, depending on their color and background color, due to the way the brain responds to color. It is all about perception. In fact, when you perceive colors, what you are really seeing is light reflected back to you in different wavelengths. These wavelengths together make up the colors of the rainbow.

Another good reason to begin with a rainbow is that it leads directly to the color wheel. This is a circle featuring the colors of the rainbow in order. The color wheel is used by designers to identify colors that harmonize, and those that don't.

Study of the color wheel gives a basic grounding in colors and how each hue relates to another one.

THE COLOR WHEEL

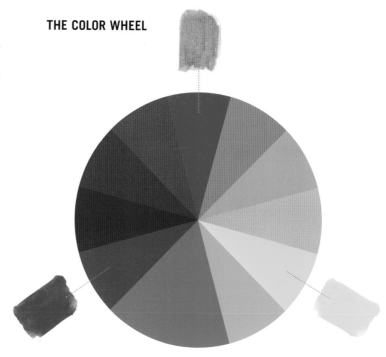

PRIMARY + PRIMARY = SECONDARY

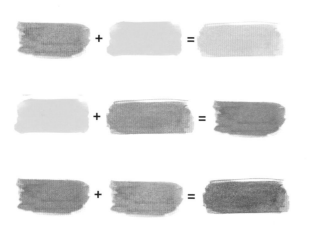

SECONDARY + PRIMARY = TERTIARY

Primary colors are the three basic colors from which all others are mixed. They are red, yellow, and blue. (See above right.)

Secondary colors are made by mixing equal amounts of the three primary colors, so red plus yellow makes orange, yellow and blue make green, and blue and red make violet. (See above.)

Tertiary colors are the hues in between the primary and secondary colors on the wheel: the mixes such as yellow-greens and red-oranges, created by blending a primary with the secondary colors on either side.

So the color wheel shows the relationships between the basic colors. Of course, there are actually an infinite number of colors, made up of all the permutations of color in between these 12. Study of the wheel helps with understanding why people perceive color combinations as pleasing or clashing, warm or cool, light or dark.

Harmonizing colors are close neighbors, such as blue and purple, on the color wheel. Harmonizing color combinations tend to have a subtle, restful effect.

Contrasting colors are from opposite sides of the color wheel: so violet and yellow, or red and green, make sizzling combinations that almost seem to be vibrating. Note how you respond differently depending on the amount of each color. (See right.)

The addition of **black and white** creates an infinite range of possibilities. Black and white are at opposite ends of the spectrum. White contains and reflects all of the other colors. In contrast, black absorbs light. The addition of white lightens colors to create, for example, pastel blues and pale pinks. Adding white creates what is known as a *tint*. The addition of black makes a *shade*, such as deep red. (See below.) Tints tend to create a feeling of airiness, whereas shades are intimate and mature.

Colors are divided into **warm and cool**, depending on the amount of hot red or cool blue they contain. (See below right.) Colors on the warm side of the wheel, such as red, orange, and yellow, seem to advance, making spaces seem smaller. Cool colors, such as blues and greens, tend to recede and give an impression of spaciousness. These properties are important as we move on to consider how to create color schemes, because colors create atmosphere and allow you to enhance or disguise the features of a room.

HARMONIZING COLORS

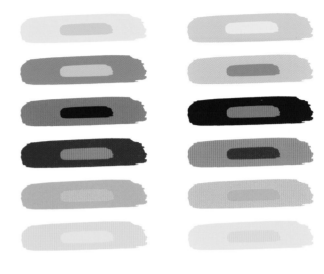

CONTRASTING COLORS

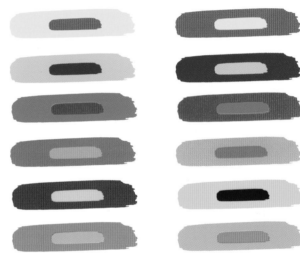

TINTS

SHADES

WARM COLORS

COOL COLORS

Above: In this welcoming family kitchen, the harmonizing warm shades of yellows and oranges have been brought to life with the dramatic contrast of royal-blue cabinets. A patterned rug and unusual accessories provide further cozy interest.

CREATING COLOR SCHEMES

A color scheme is a set of colors that creates a pleasing effect, whether it's dramatic or pretty. Many decorators follow the simple rule of using two main harmonizing colors, probably on the walls and flooring, and then enlivening the scheme with small amounts of contrasting accent color throughout the room, often in the soft furnishings and accessories. But many of the best schemes break these rules to dramatic effect.

A vital concept when putting together a scheme is *tonal value*. Imagine a black and white photograph of a room you know. Any colors that are the same shade of gray have similar value, because this is the term for how light or dark a color is. The tonal values chosen for a room set the mood. A set of similar tonal values and similar colors can create a dull, flat impression: tonal contrast adds depth and interest.

Darker tones appear to bring surfaces closer to us—and so can make a high ceiling seem lower, or a large room more cozy, for example. Lighter tones reflect more light and thus create distance, which can be good for making small areas seem larger.

Many people are worried about mixing colors and often stick to monochromatic schemes, which use just one hue—such as blue or green—sometimes in different shades. A monochromatic scheme can be highly successful, particularly when it makes clever use of tone. But don't be afraid to play around with colors. Harmonizing schemes are relaxing and easy to live with, but they can look monotonous without a little contrast. The addition of a small amount of contrasting accent color accentuates the quality of the other hues and enlivens the scheme.

Creating a contrasting scheme by mixing colors from opposite sides of the wheel, even combining cool and warm hues, can have exciting effects. Be aware of your color proportions—the quantity of any color used will affect the overall look. Orange pillows used as an accent in a blue scheme will have quite a different impact than a bold orange feature wall.

Don't forget about pattern and texture: large areas of flat color can be dull and even overpowering. Perhaps consider a textured paint effect or textured rugs and pillows. The texture of unpainted wood will have quite a different effect from sleek glass or steel. The simpler your color choices, the more your room may benefit from dramatic texture. When considering pattern, your choices may be dictated by the rugs or curtains you already own. Patterns will affect the perception of your scheme, whether it's bold geometrics enlivening a pastel scheme, or pretty florals softening a stark neutral look.

What Does the Room Need?

When you are planning your color scheme, the first thing to do is decide on your priorities:

- Consider the size and proportions of the room: do you want to adjust them through color? For example, does the room seem narrow, or the ceiling too high?

Above: A rich red is contrasted with stark white and black here. This look plays creatively with both contrast and tone. The coffered ceiling becomes a focal point with dramatic color and paint.

Below: This cozy den takes its inspiration from India. Saffron walls are pleasingly contrasted with a scarlet carpet for a warm and friendly feel. Accessories continue the exotic theme: an Indian-style print, rug, and wall-hanging; colored-glass and metalwork lamps; and carved-wood furniture.

Left: This huge living area is made cozy by the use of warm yellow and terra-cotta flooring. Accent is provided by hot-pink pillows and subtle blues in the soft furnishings. The effect is sunny and Mediterranean.

Finding Inspiration

You may already have an idea for a color or effect that you would like to be the centerpiece of your room. Another good starting point is a piece of fabric or a pattern that you particularly like, in which case use some of the colors in it to kick off your scheme. For further inspiration:

- Collect manufacturers' paint chips so that you can set colors side by side. Retailers are also able to mix paint to match your own sample—take this book into the store and see what they can do. Buy a small sample.
- Keep a file of colors and textures that you like, taken from magazines or paintings.
- Get small swatches of fabric from stores.
- Turn to history for inspiration. (See "Period Colors," page 133.) First consider when your house was built—a neoclassical scheme may work less well in a postmodern apartment.
- Study nature for ideas. Color schemes in the natural world are vibrant and extraordinary—think of the rich green of mosses with the gold-red of fall leaves, turquoise seas and sandy beaches, garden flowers and new leaves. Or turn to the urban environment—do you like the way steel looks against wood, or the way red roofs contrast with stone. What sort of environment do you want to create with color?
- For a children's bedroom or nursery, look to their interests and favorite books for ideas.

- Think about what style suits you and the room: modern minimalist, rural retreat, elegant, traditional floral? Your decision may be dictated by the architectural style of the room and any period features, such as a fireplace.
- Do you want to make the room feel warm, elegant, cool, cozy, uncluttered?
- Are there any features or shapes in the room that you want to draw attention to or hide? Accent colors will show them off, while the use of similar tones will disguise them.
- To ensure a balanced effect or to create a focus, decide whether you want to emphasize the background or the furnishings.
- How does the natural light fall in the room and do you want to accentuate it or make it more mellow? A north-facing room may need brightening with a light floor or sunny-colored walls.
- Think of the room layout and where the furniture will be—the largest unadorned area will be the ceiling.

Once you have chosen your scheme, pin the color swatches and any fabric samples onto a board. Try looking at the board in the room where the colors will be used, in both natural and artificial light. This is your chance to experiment—you can change your mind now without wasting a drop of paint.

Consider how the color schemes of each room in your home can be related: a doorway revealing a very different range of colors in an adjacent space can create a jarring effect and closes off the area, making the home seem smaller. Maybe you could use the same flooring or wall color in adjoining areas?

Right: In this child's bedroom, a fanciful medieval joust has been painted on the walls. Find inspiration for children's rooms in their favorite pastimes and interests, whether that's animals, sports, or a storybook.

CHOOSING PAINT EFFECTS

There is a wealth of ways to apply paint to create special effects. If you want to add interest to an area that is to be painted, use the "Choosing Paint Techniques" section of this book, which begins on page 174. If you want to bring that special touch of originality by painting images onto the wall, see "Making Pictures," beginning on page 176, which details techniques such as trompe l'oeil, stenciling, and painting a fresco. In "Textural Finishes," starting on page 192, you will find a guide to effects such as ageing (to give the paint surface the look of a well-loved antique), colorwashing (which softens and adds depth to large expanses of wall), the randomly patterned finishes of ragging or sponging, and the dramatic rhythmic look offered by stippling. "Faux Techniques," beginning on page 208, describes effects such as bronzing, marbling, rusting, and wood graining. They are terrific ways to add texture, interest, and grandeur.

DO IT YOURSELF?

Once you have planned your color scheme, you need to decide if you are going to do the painting yourself or hire a professional. If you've decided on a paint effect, the "Do it yourself?" feature in each section will help you decide whether you're up to the task. While doing your own painting will certainly save money, it demands skill, commitment, and, above all, time. A professional will probably do the job faster, and will have the experience to complete the essential preparation work efficiently and achieve a high-quality finish.

Before employing a professional, you need to know exactly what you want, so that you can convey it accurately and judge the quality of the work. To help you with this, the "Practical Checklist," beginning on page 226, has tips for dealing with professionals and sticking to a budget. This section also briefs you on what kinds of paint you can use and how much you need to load into your shopping cart.

So you've got guidance on how to devise your own color schemes, the opportunity to see many different ways in which rooms can be decorated, and advice on how to achieve the effects you want. Happy painting!

Above: This guest bathroom would be plain and featureless without the pearlized effect on the walls, which creates texture and light. The contrasting colors of mauve and dull green are used to dramatic effect.

Choosing Color

Sometimes the wide choice of colors that is available to you can be overwhelming, especially in the absence of some established pattern or feature that could provide your starting point. The following chapters will help you to make your color-scheme choices. They will give you the opportunity to study the same room set in a multitude of different colors so that you can decide what you like. Also, each chapter contains inspirational photographs that are divided into color groups and followed by clear illustrations showing the palette on its own and combined with its harmonizing and contrasting partners.

Naturals and Neutrals

The natural colors of sand, stone, sky, leaves, or driftwood are ideal for rooms where the interest is focused on an architectural detail, pattern, or texture. But naturals are not just a superb backdrop—they can form a sophisticated scheme in their own right.

Opposite: Neutrals and naturals are perfect for updating classic architectural details, such as this fireplace, with a contemporary look. Heather on the walls teamed with sky blue on the painted wooden floor creates a calming, warm ambiance for this bedroom.

Most people feel at home with natural materials, such as wood and stone, because these materials form the structures they inhabit. The natural palette is made up of off-whites, a subtle range of creams, earthy browns of all shades, and all the sophisticated grays. Joining them in offering a neutral canvas are pale and dark blues that reflect the many moods of the sky, all the greens you might see in an abundant forest, and the numerous yellows of the sun.

In the eighteenth and nineteenth centuries, most interiors were painted so-called "drab" gray. The Georgians often teamed gray with an elegant cream for their trademark neutral look. They subtly highlighted architectural detailing by accenting it in narrowly differentiated neutral shades. Woodwork, such as doors and paneling, was kept neutral brown, reflecting its natural origins.

Dark naturals can add depth and drama to a setting. Light naturals are cooler and tend to look more contemporary. Naturals soften hard lines in a room, bringing a sense of space and calm. Warm shades, such as ivory and copper, combine well with cool naturals, such as sandstone and gray. Indeed, naturals work well together, especially when they are used together with white and black to offset stronger colors such as deep red and warm blues. Avoid blandness by blending light, medium, and dark tones, especially if you are using only one base color. Try adding texture with paint techniques, such as ragging, sponging, and stippling.

Materials that harmonize well with these neutral hues are also natural. Look at pale wood floors together with other natural woods, cork, pebbles, sisal, leather, linen, earthenware pots, bamboo, and wicker.

These photographs illustrate the roles of neutral colors: providing a setting for other hues or textures to take the stage, or bringing unity to a room while adding a touch of warmth or sophistication. However, it is still important to choose neutral backdrop colors wisely and aim for harmony rather than discordant clashes from competing elements.

Above: The warm mushroom wall and natural-wood floor are enlivened by the fuchsia pink bed and welcoming striped coverlet. Wicker accents and linen shades keep to the natural theme.

Above: A cream-painted desk and wall provide a neutral backdrop that harmonizes well with the leaf-green chair and shelving unit.

Above: This sophisticated bathroom uses warm neutrals of stone and sand to strong effect.

Left: This light, elegant room combines ivory walls and curtains with a coffee color in the furnishings and rug border.

Below: Stripes and textures combine well with an understated natural scheme of apple green and pale stone.

Above: Neutrals are the classic choice for a restful, practical bathroom. Here a golden cream works with natural wood.

Above: Bold yellow and red pillows and chairs pop against the striped sea-blue sofa, cream walls, and natural floor.

Above: Pale aqua walls and white-painted floorboards create a relaxed, natural look. The accessories are kept simple.

Above: This bedroom teams a warm chocolate brown with the contrasting shades of gold and green. The sheepskin coverlet provides texture.

Above: This period room combines a strong, flat gray-blue with cream. Brick and natural wood complete the simple effect.

Above: Naturals can be dramatic when used boldly with clean lines and modern furniture. In this contemporary living room, a warm China blue is teamed with slate, stone, and wood.

Color Palette

Despite their apparent simplicity, many neutrals are in fact complex mixes of a range of hues. Take nature as your base, and choose from off-white, creams, yellows, browns, grays, blues, and greens. It's easy to live with these colors because they do not overwhelm other colors or compete with subtle textures.

Hints of color

Creams

Sands

Café au laits

Chocolates

Sky grays

Steel grays

Sky blues

Deep blues

Fresh greens

Moss greens

Warm yellows

Harmonious Schemes

Harmonizing naturals and neutrals with each other allows you to explore variations on a theme, maintaining interest and avoiding the blandness of the repeated use of just one color. Think of nature when creating your schemes—try mixing sea and sand, bark and leaves, stone and moss.

Hint of color and mist blue

Cream and coffee

Sand and pale green

Café au lait and rust

Chocolate, cream, and mint

Sky gray, dark gray, and pale blue

Steel gray, white, and blue

Sky blue, lilac, and heather

Deep blue, pale blue, and lilac

Fresh greens and brown

Moss green and stone

Warm yellow, mushroom, and saffron

Contrasting Schemes

For more vitality in your scheme, or to draw the eye to favorite features, introduce contrasting hues to your natural palette. For the best effects, turn to nature's contrasts—think of exotic blooms among rainforest foliage, rich spices with stone, strawberries with cream.

Hint of color and green

Cream and lime

Sand and blues

Café au lait and saffron

Chocolate and pink

Sky gray and maroon

Steel gray and turquoise

Sky blue and lemon

Deep blues, gold, and white

Fresh green and fuchsia

Moss green, brown, and scarlet

Yellow, peach, and olive

The same room can take on a variety of moods when colored differently, even when all the hues are neutrals and naturals. This simply decorated bedroom can look feminine or masculine, modern or traditional, vibrant or relaxed, while never leaving the palette. Keeping to a limited neutral palette, with its slate-gray bedding, stark ivory walls, and cream carpet, the bedroom pictured above has a classically masculine feel.

1 Chocolate brown on the feature wall makes a strong statement, balanced by the warm tones of the coffee bedding and cream carpet.

2 Sage green harmonizes well with brown, while the café au lait on the walls lifts the eyes away from the darker carpet, making the room seem larger.

3 Attention is focused on the inviting raspberry-red bed by contrasting it with the pale-gray carpet and neutral stone-color walls.

4 White walls offer a refreshing contrast to the mint green bedding and heather feature wall, which blend with the gray carpet for a serene feel.

5 Deep-red pillows demonstrate how powerful a contrasting accent color can be when it's used sparingly with soft neutrals of a similar tonal value.

6 Shades of soft green are harmonized for a classic feminine effect: gray-green walls, shoot-green pillows, and palest-green bedding and carpet.

7 Here is a trio of harmonizing colors: the dominant dark-green bedding links the pale-green carpet and the warm terra-cotta wall.

8 A rich deep blue creates a luxurious bed, harmonizing with gray-blue in the carpet and ivory on the walls for a bold, modern bedroom.

9 The walls are painted in a gray off-white, picked up by the steel-gray carpet. The effect is enlivened by the emerald bedding.

1 Wood and cream create a warm, welcoming effect. The natural dark wood of the baseboard and door frames acts as a unifying feature.

2 Two neutrals in subtly different tones allow the brilliant white woodwork to shine. The reflective quality of the white makes the small hallway seem airy.

3 Mushroom is the dominant color on the wall and doors, providing a calm setting for the strongly contrasting aqua woodwork.

Hallways and central areas should look warm and welcoming while blending with the decor of the adjoining rooms that are visible from these areas. Hallways are a perfect place to experiment with the neutral and natural palette to understated effect. In the pictured hallway, natural wood blended with chocolate walls and black woodwork creates a traditional yet bold feel.

4 Painting all the woodwork, including the bannister, forest green makes a strong statement, offset by the much lighter tint on the wall.

5 Dark floors and light walls bring a sense of space. Here the ivory walls and pale-green doors create a contemporary effect.

6 Gray walls are here harmonized with turquoise doors and stairway, and teamed with pale blue-gray floorboards, for a quiet and calm feel.

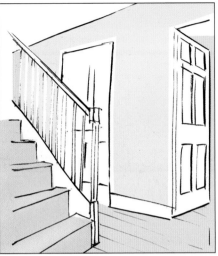

7 Gray is the purest neutral, perfectly balanced between black and white. Here it combines with pale blue to create a sophisticated feel.

8 Soft pink walls contrast with the natural-oak woodwork and the bleached-wood flooring. The overall effect is warm and enticing.

9 Bold aqua bannisters and doors are subtly harmonized with leaf-green baseboards. Gray walls are lightened by stark white floorboards.

Pretty Pastels

The light, gentle touch of pastels creates a restful atmosphere, and can make small or dark rooms feel larger and more airy. Pastels are traditionally feminine shades, but they don't have to be confined just to the bedroom or teamed with the same old florals.

Pastels are pure colors mixed with white. Because of their common white base, pastels don't clash with each other, and work well together as a color family. Vivid colors that would otherwise be over-dominant, such as a lime green or fuchsia pink, can—with the crucial addition of white— become fresh and calm, while retaining some of the vibrancy of the base color.

If you find pastels overly sweet, team them with deep, natural colors, such as dark blue or forest green, for a more sophisticated and dramatic effect. If you would like to keep the look from becoming too feminine, use a mix of contrasting pastel shades, and then team them with a bold accent color or even bright white. The grayer shades of pastels can be matched with cool, strong colors, such as blue. Very white pastels can lack depth and benefit from a warm, heavy accent color such as red.

Although their soft and gentle touch makes them compatible with bedrooms, pastels work well in other parts of the house, too. In living rooms, where many homeowners prefer a color that is easy on the eye, neutral pastels— such as pale green, sky blue, or dove gray—work very well. When used in a kitchen, pastels are ideal for softening, and can be used to striking effect in the most hard-edged modern kitchens.

The look you create with your pastel color scheme can be as traditional or as bold as you like— depending on your soft furnishing, furniture, and accessory choices. Teaming pastels with glass, chrome, and other reflective surfaces creates a pleasing balance of masculine and feminine. Soft furnishings making use of stripes and geometric patterns can be alternatives to modern florals. Rustic or cottage furniture is a pretty, traditional partner for pastels.

Opposite: This traditional living room has been made delicate and light with its subtle combination of pastel shades. Palest aqua on the walls is picked up with mint woodwork, while the warm pinks of the soft furnishings provide a refreshing contrast.

Pastels make good companions for many colors, from calming neutrals to brilliant blues and reds. In fact, pastels are one of the most adaptable color families and can be put to great effect in the most utilitarian office or a comfortable den. They can be used in period schemes, from Art Deco to Colonial, or soften a cutting-edge, contemporary look.

Below: In this cool, refreshing bathroom, lemon has been paired with white gloss latex paint on the woodwork.

Above: Pastels can be used to soften the hard lines of a kitchen. Here the jade-painted cabinets offer a refreshing contrast to the natural wood of the countertop.

Above: A vibrant lime pastel, teamed with white woodwork, creates a modern and welcoming feel in this breakfast area.

Left: Stripes of pastel lemon and bolder sunshine yellow create a zesty contrast.

Above: Different pastel blues combine to create a warm but contemporary unified look.

Above: Pastels are ideal for brightening a rustic style. Here a willow-green bed is matched with a pretty pastel-patterned quilt.

Below: Tints of lemon, dusty pink, and soft apple green are echoed around this warm and restful sitting room.

Below: Here a vibrant blue pastel contrasts with a soft strawberry pink, while natural wood floors and cream walls provide a backdrop.

Left: Pastels are ideal for softening an otherwise workaday setting. This simple office is made peaceful by its pastel-green walls and dove-blue blinds.

Above: Cream walls are easy on the eye while a leaf-green sofa and fuchsia rug lift the room.

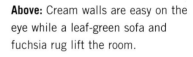

Left: This fresh leaf green contrasts perfectly with dark, natural wood and the refreshing chintz of the chair covering.

Color Palette

The pastel color family is soft and pretty, but can bring character to a room, as well. The pinks are warm and welcoming, the blues are quietly assertive, and the greens are vibrant and refreshing. Pastels allow you to use a wide palette without the look becoming too strident.

Pastel whites

Lemons

Pale pinks

Warm pinks

Peaches

Baby blues

Sky blues

Lilacs

Pale greens

Dusty greens

Pastel grays

Turquoises

Harmonious Schemes

The right blend of harmonizing pastels prevents them from becoming overly sweet. These restful combinations are easy on the eye without being dull. White, on woodwork or soft furnishings, makes a stark accent for schemes using combinations of pastels, while natural wood, wicker, and other natural textures can finish the look.

Pastel whites and baby blue

Lemon and vanilla

Pale pink and lilac

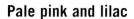

Warm pink, cream, and chocolate

Peach and strawberry

Pale blue, mauve, and cream

Sky blue, royal blue, and pink

Lilac and hot pink

Pale green, turquoise, and cream

Dusty green, forest green, and blue

Pastel gray and lilac

Turquoise and navy

Contrasting Schemes

Pastels can get a huge lift when paired with contrasting colors, creating modern, vibrant, and sometimes surprising schemes. Cool pastels can be teamed pleasingly with hot pink or sizzling orange, while warm pinks or yellows are dramatic with royal blue or deep green.

Pastel whites and fuchsia

Lemon and royal blue

Pale pink, dark green, and brown

Warm pink, mauve, and leaf green

Peach and purple

Pale blue, pale green, and strawberry

Sky blue and orange

Lilac and bottle green

Pale green, lemon, and walnut

Dusty green and peach

Pastel gray, hot pink, and purple

Turquoise, gold, and navy blue

1 The lilac of the furnishings is accented by olive pillows. Baby-blue walls and wooden floors provide refreshing contrast.

2 This modern pastel scheme combines pale strawberry walls with leaf-green furnishings, hot-pink pillows, and natural wood floors.

A living room is an ideal place to play around with pastels for a welcoming feel. In a small living area, it is worth considering how cool colors recede and warm colors advance to dramatically alter the perceived room size. Wooden floors can be painted to harmonize or contrast with other elements in the scheme. In the room pictured above, a restrained pastel scheme of pale lemon walls, aqua baseboards, and an ivory chair, is contrasted with fuchsia and purple pillows.

3 The blue floor, white paintwork, beige furnishings, and lilac walls create an airy scheme.

4 This dramatic use of pastel lemon is striking and contemporary. Burnt-orange pillows and stark white floorboards provide a bold accent.

7 Pastel-blue walls are teamed with a China blue in this subtle monochromatic scheme. Natural wood floors and white paintwork provide tonal variation.

5 This luxurious, feminine look is created with harmonies of warm pastel pink, deep purple, and hot scarlet pillows. Natural floorboards prevent overkill.

8 For an intimate, comforting room, experiment with a combination of naturals and pastels, such as toffee, biscuit, café au lait, and palest strawberry.

6 This scheme contrasts apple green with a rich purple for a modern look.

9 Apple green and lemon are a refreshing pairing, particularly when teamed with bright white.

When devising a color scheme, determine whether there are features of the room that you would like to accentuate or disguise. The choice in this room is whether to allow the large window areas to dominate (through the use of contrast between walls and shutters) or to draw attention toward the center of the room. This pastel scheme gives the impression that the room is bathed in sunlight with its use of lemon walls, sandy shutters, lime sofas, and contrasting navy pillows.

1 The room appears to have doubled in size with the introduction of a white-painted floor and cool-blue walls. The deep-blue sofa and candy pillows invite relaxation.

2 This mature pastel scheme has turned to nature for inspiration: heather walls, forest-green sofas, leaf-green pillows, and natural wood flooring.

3 Palest apricot walls are teamed with baby-blue flooring, hard-wearing mauve-gray sofas, and contrasting bottle-green pillows.

6 Pastels can be dramatic, as the lemon walls set against lime-green shutters demonstrate. Mustard sofas and saffron pillows pick up the bold theme.

4 The focus here is on the pink sofa with hot geranium cushions, teamed with a chocolate carpet and palest salmon walls.

7 Citrus-yellow walls and a white-painted floor open up the room. Pale-blue sofas and purple pillows provide a surprisingly bold contrast.

5 The contrast between the sky-blue walls and the soft-pink shutters highlights the size of the windows.

8 This pretty scheme of white, apple green, and lilac creates a feeling of space.

Warm and Cozy

The colors of a warm palette make spaces seem inviting and intimate yet stimulating and opulent. By day they are open and welcoming, then they graduate into something excitingly sensuous and spicy as the light fades toward evening.

Opposite: The warm pink used on the walls of this inviting bedroom is a complex shade, falling somewhere between soft mauve and hot fuchsia. It forms a rich backdrop for the Victorian fireplace and teams well with the natural textures of wicker and unpainted wood.

The colors in this palette all fall on the warm side of the color wheel (see page 9). The warmth of the color is dependent on the amount of red in the mix: pinky purples are more vibrant and energetically welcoming than those with a higher proportion of cooling blue, for example. For inspiration, turn to spices—think of saffron, cinnamon, and paprika.

Deep warm colors create a cheery, cozy feel, so they are particularly suited to large rooms, which can otherwise appear cold and unwelcoming. With their suggestion of sunny climes, paler warm shades, such as yellow, work well in rooms that get little light.

This palette has historically been popular in living and dining rooms and more formal areas such as studies and libraries, but it can work very well in kitchens, too, softening hard lines. These highly practical shades resist wear, tear, and dirt, too.

Exotic, rich colors, such as cinnamon and dusky purple, can bring a sense of grown-up glamor to your rooms. The more frivolous shades in this palette, such as pinks, can be rendered more serious when paired with chocolate brown or burgundy. This is a thoroughly mature color range.

Because of their power, these colors like to be balanced by elements of equal character in the room, such as architectural moldings or fireplaces, warm metallic lamps, or burnished bronze sculptures. Textures that work well are rich but simple: dark mahogany wood, stone, and brick. For soft furnishings, think of highly patterned Turkish rugs, rich damasks, and deep velvets.

A color wash or stippled paint effect is useful for adding texture to these shades, especially when using earthy relations of terracotta, such as warm brown or dark orange.

This color palette does more than bring character and intimacy to a room: it is particularly suited to blending the past with the present. Ornate gold fittings such as chandeliers or mirrors, or dark-wood antique furniture, all benefit from this softening yet luxurious backdrop. Boldly mix these powerful colors with other strong shades for maximum impact.

Above: The warmth of the ocher walls is pleasingly teamed with plenty of cool greenery and heavy dark wood.

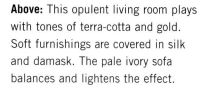

Above: This opulent living room plays with tones of terra-cotta and gold. Soft furnishings are covered in silk and damask. The pale ivory sofa balances and lightens the effect.

Above: The saffron of the walls is cleverly echoed by leopard and red-velvet soft furnishings. The eclectic mixture of Empire-style accessories creates a sophisticated but playful feel.

Above: A mellow red wall softens the functional lines in this bathroom. The incandescent lighting enhances warm colors in a way that fluorescent lighting cannot.

Right: Two shades of yellow combine to create a feeling of sunlight and Mediterranean days. The apple green woodwork and red pillows balance the scheme.

Below: Matching the ceiling with the plush lilac of the walls unifies the room and sets off the neoclassical-style gold detailing.

Above: In this small dining area, the light is softened and the room looks airier with sunny tones of yellow and cream.

Above: Strong red walls, teamed with bright sunflowers, dark wood, and antique accessories, make this cottage-style living area deliciously inviting.

Above: The decor in this room is focused on the warm tones of the brickwork fireplace, echoed by the burgundy walls, and lifted by the yellows and pale blue-green of the furnishings.

Left: If you own a favorite quilt or rug, it can become the centerpiece of your decorating scheme. This quilt's rich, warm tones are picked up in the deep pink of the walls.

Color Palette

These cheery colors invite you into the room. The many variations of yellow offer a neutral but sunny backdrop, while the deeper and stronger pinks, reds, and purples make a powerful statement. The shades of chocolate brown are particularly effective in nineteenth-century-style decor.

Warm creams

Sands

Sunshine yellows

Tawny oranges

Burnt oranges

Peaches

Pinks

Hot pinks

Reds

Purples

Aubergines

Chocolates

Harmonious Schemes

Mixing together the shades on the warm side of the color wheel (see page 9) creates harmonizing, hospitable color schemes, which can be hot and spicy (as with red, brown, and orange) or subtle (tawny orange, peach, and burgundy, for example).

Warm cream, pink, and lilac

Sands and terra-cotta

Sunshine yellow, orange, and olive

Tawny orange, peach, and burgundy

Burnt orange and pink

Peach, orange, and brown

Pink, red, and cream

Hot pink, indigo, and gray-blue

Red, brown, and orange

Purple, royal blue, and pale lilac

Aubergine and blue

Chocolate, orange, and mushroom

Contrasting Schemes

Contrasting warm shades with splashes of cool color from the other side of the color wheel creates balanced and subtle schemes. Black, white, and cream also act as superb contrasting foils to warm shades. Greens, such as moss and lime, are especially happy to cohabit with cozy colors.

Warm cream, chocolate, and olive

Sand and mauve

Sunshine yellow, purple, and pink

Tawny oranges and black

Burnt orange and violet

Peach and moss green

Pink, mint, and lilac

Hot pink and lime

Red, terra-cotta, and blue

Purple, sand, and mint

Aubergine, moss, and pink

Chocolate, terra-cotta, and mauve

1 Coloring a recessed wall a darker color creates a sense of depth. Here the warm palette is used subtly, creating coziness without overpowering.

2 Orange was a very popular color in Art Deco decoration, and often paired with pink and purple for interest.

3 Painting a favorite architectural feature a warm shade, such as ocher, creates a focal point.

Fireplaces form a natural focus for the room—and rooms with hearths are ideal for experimenting with a warm, welcoming palette. If a living area lacks natural light, use lighter tones to brighten it. Darker colors will make a large room feel more intimate. Painting walls contrasting colors adds interest. Here the rusty scarlet of the feature wall focuses attention firmly on the fireplace.

4 The whole range of warm shades is on display here, from the pale-pink carpet to the aubergine walls, creating complex harmonies.

5 This dark purple feature wall would be overpowering if it were not paired with magenta and softening neutral brown flooring.

6 Scarlet is a classic color for living rooms. Here it's teamed with orange, white, and beige.

7 The neoclassical burgundy of the walls is here given a modern twist with a restrained splash of vibrant saffron and orange.

8 Mustard on the feature wall contrasts with cooler mauve on the opposing wall, both strong colors that are balanced by the neutral browns of the floor.

9 This neutral scheme is made cozy and welcoming by the addition of orange accents.

1 Rich burgundy on the walls and the dark-brown doors harmonize with the pale-pink carpeting—anything darker here would be forbidding.

2 Blood-red carpeting complements the burnt-orange walls and sandy doors, creating a modern, bright space.

3 Pale-pink walls team well with the rose carpet and cream woodwork, for a fresh, soft look.

To welcome visitors into your home, try experimenting with the warm palette in your entranceway. Many entranceways have a paucity of natural light, which can be ameliorated by the sunny effects of cozy shades. Bear in mind that a vibrant hallway runs the risk of clashing with adjoining rooms, so keep your palette limited. In the scheme above, warm terra-cotta on the walls harmonizes well with the natural oak of the doors. The tiled floors and traditional furniture complete the classic look.

4 Warm cream walls and floors are a classic choice. Here they are enlivened by dark-red woodwork, linking the hallway with the stairs and balustrade.

5 Pink hues are always friendly—and here the use of a variety of tones creates interest. The bright white flooring and woodwork supply contrast.

6 The shades of orange and dusty peach create a warm and sunny harmony.

7 The mustard color could be overpowering if it were not for the neutral carpet and white woodwork. The effect is sophisticated and bold.

8 Chocolate brown on the woodwork harmonizes with the cream carpet, while yellow walls add daring contrast.

9 This otherwise neutral scheme is brought to life by the cozy orange of the carpet.

Hot Housing

The key to hot housing is the invigorating use of blocks of hot hues, often boldly contrasting with each other. Using bright, strong colors can make a room sparkle. This wild look isn't for everyone—but used with care *and* dare, hot housing can bring fun into your home.

Opposite: Wooden flooring and white baseboards balance the bold, matte colors. The orange walls sizzle with the scarlet dining chairs. The blue sofas cool the effect while complementing the tangerine glow of the footstool. The effect is bravely modern.

Many people worry that hot colors are garish and overwhelming, but this need not be the case. Bold colors—of flowers, midday skies, new leaves—abound in nature, and the effect is vitality, not vulgarity. Travel this daring route and you follow in the footsteps of the French Sun King Louis XIV, Indian maharajahs, and designers from the psychedelic 1960s.

Blocks of hot color can help to define the space in a room and make it look clean and bright, while retaining energy. Hot colors are perfect for family-friendly dens, children's rooms, daring dining areas, and welcoming kitchens. Any busy, active room can handle these exotic, daring shades, especially if it is north or east facing and suffers from poor natural light.

If you'd like to prevent your scheme from becoming too loud, don't water down the colors by making some of the shades pastel. Rather, put hot colors with white and off-white or a natural shade that will keep the volume down yet retain the pure feel. Try painting the ceiling, woodwork, and architectural details in shades of white to give the eye a rest. Cream sofas have the same impact.

Hot colors complement natural wood finishes very well with a Caribbean look: pale wooden flooring, unvarnished wood furniture, and oiled wood accessories blend with the strongest tropical hues. Linear, hard-edged furniture and glass can create a more audacious modern feel. You can maintain the balance in the room by adding subtle texture through deep-pile rugs, the matte finishes of soft cottons and linens, and natural materials such as bamboo and stone. If it's a Bollywood look you're after, go the whole way with shiny silks and satins, floating muslins, gold, silver, and sequins.

Intense colors bring relief from the daily grind. All these rooms call on bold, dynamic hues to energize their spaces. Too many accessories or competing colors will turn the area into a battlefield: neutral tones and natural surfaces, such as stone, wood, and linen, are used to complement the dramatic colors on the walls.

Above: Painting just one wall a hot color stops the effect from overwhelming the room.

Above: The hot-pink wall contrasts boldly with a bright-blue rug, while sinuous accessories and a well-chosen painting complete the cutting-edge effect.

Above: Orange, red, and yellow applied imaginatively make this kitchen glow with warmth and energy. White trim and silver accessories keep it grounded.

Left: Tomato-red walls are echoed in the checked Roman blind. The mixture of colors used on the chairs is pleasingly informal but unified.

Left: Tropical blue and lime are accented by bright yellows, creating a relaxed Indian-style feel.

Color Palette

Hot colors evoke the vitality of a South American fiesta or an Indian street market. The standout colors are the fiery reds, which awaken the senses and stimulate the palette (which is why reds are used so much for restaurant decor). Each of these hues is extravagant, and generous yet sophisticated.

Limes

Bright yellows

Bright pinks

Hot oranges

Turquoises

Violets

Metallic blues

Deep greens

Cherry reds

Acid pinks

Deep blues

Lemons

Harmonious Schemes

Naturals and neutrals form a great balancing act with hot colors, but there are some other interesting variations here. Use darker shades such as violet, navy, and pink in sunnier rooms, but combine yellows and blues to lift darker areas. Hot pink mixes well with other tropical hues, such as orange.

Lime and white

Bright yellow and scarlet

Bright pink and pale pink

Hot orange, fuchsia, and indigo

Turquoise and sky blue

Violet, navy, and pink

Metallic blue and purple

Deep green, lime, and sand

Cherry red, orange, and peach

Acid pink and softer pinks

Deep blue and mauves

Lemon, mustard, and white

Contrasting Schemes

Contrasting hot shades add vitality to busy and sociable areas. Mixing hot and cool colors from opposite sides of the color wheel (see page 9) can create interesting spacial effects: cool colors recede and warm colors advance. The result of these contrasting combinations is daring and fun.

Lime and pink

Bright yellow, turquoise, and brown

Bright pink, black, and violet

Hot orange and olive

Turquoise and lemon

Violet and forest green

Metallic blue and orange

Deep green and pink

Cherry red, pink, and green

Acid pink and saffron

Deep blue, hot pink, and gray

Lemon and lime

1 The burnt orange of the walls is an excellent meeting point for the dynamic red and yellow.

This bold 1960s-style sitting area uses an inviting hot-pink carpet teamed with pale-pink walls and a strongly patterned sofa. The Andy Warhol print of Marilyn Monroe on the wall demonstrates the graphic power of bold colors that are used together. The following variations on a red color scheme show that no shade matches its drama and energy.

2 Bluish shades of purple and pink on the walls leave the passionate red of the sofa to shine.

3 Brown provides a firm base for the exotic fuchsia of the sofa and its complementing pink walls.

4 Harmonizing orange and saffron walls contrast with the inviting scarlet sofa.

7 A tangerine sofa and cherry-red walls are contrasted with a white floor, which allows the room to breathe.

5 Rooms with hot colors respond well to bold pattern. Here bright pink contrasts with a gray carpet.

8 This daring scheme uses two challenging colors in perfect combination: icy white and fiery red.

6 Pink, purple, and yellow provide a sizzling and daring combination.

9 This scheme of white teamed with brights focuses attention on the sofa and the orange feature wall.

A dining area is a good place to play with a dramatic color scheme. While red is the perfect color for formal dining, zesty lime is bright and enlivening in this more relaxed dining corner, while vivacious turquoise provides a sociable contrast. The fresh curtains and natural wood give an airy feel.

1 Pineapple yellow and lime green create a refreshing casual dining area, contrasted with natural wood and white.

2 Pale-yellow curtains prevent the banana of the feature wall from overpowering the room, as does the white contrasting wall.

3 This color scheme is more dramatic than it looks at first glance: white-painted walls contrast playfully with tropical-stripe curtains.

6 Bright-yellow curtains contrast with stark white walls and natural wood floors for a modern but warm feel.

4 The balance of warm chocolate brown, cool turquoise, and rich, romantic purple makes this an opulent dining area.

7 Saturated pink and a more traditional forest green is a subtle combination that blends drama with sophistication.

5 The red element in this shade of purple is important for adding warmth to this dining area.

8 Tangerine and turquoise offer a sizzling combination, teamed with burnt-orange curtains.

Kitchens are often starved of color—but hot housing is particularly suited to these central areas, where a lively, cheerful feel is ideal. Blocks of strong color can accentuate the sharp lines of a modern kitchen, creating a dramatic contemporary look. Here bold matte red on the cabinets is contrasted with bright white walls, shining stainless steel, black countertops, and slate flooring.

1 The pale blue is calm and uncluttered, while the darker shade defines the space very clearly. Blue and white is a classic partnership for kitchens and dinnerware.

2 Red and green walls with a black floor create a retro feel, harking back to diners of the 1950s.

3 The attention-grabbing orange and yellow walls are balanced by the simple tan cabinets and beige floor.

6 The citrus-green on the walls is appropriate for a kitchen, while contrasting with the royal-blue cabinets.

4 Yellow is cheery and invigorating. Paired with white, it is sure to give you a lift at breakfast every morning. Soft lighting will make it mellow for the evening.

7 The dark green contrasts strongly with the dramatic white of the floor and walls for a zesty feel.

5 A dark floor makes the space intimate, balanced by the cool harmonizing shades of blue on the walls.

8 The red cabinets harmonize with the bright orange walls for a cozy family kitchen.

Mediterranean Magic

The Mediterranean palette comes from the sea, sky, sun, and earth. All the blues of the sea and air combine with the many yellow moods and shades of the sun, sitting comfortably with the heat-fired colors of terra-cotta and burnt orange.

The inspiration for the Mediterranean look is the homes of Italy and Greece. Built and painted to be cool and comfortable in the blazing summer sun, they have reflective white exterior walls and woodwork painted an insect-repellent blue. But this look is not just for hot locales. It can bring a touch of warmth into a cold climate, while the natural terra-cottas and sunshine yellows of the palette offer year-round coziness. The look is rustic, but with the sophistication offered by a palette that is very sure of its effect.

Blue is the essential element of a Mediterranean scheme, sometimes as the dominant color and sometimes as an accent in shades of azure or turquoise. Blue's most common partner is yellow, with which blue can seem playful and informal but sometimes electrically exciting. The classic backdrop to these colors is usually the mellow tones

of terra-cotta. This pairs happily with the earthy colors of red, orange, and ocher. Fundamental to the Mediterranean look is the contrast of cool and warm colors, such as blue with terra-cotta. It is this traditional pairing that allows both a feeling of coolness in summer and a cozy warmth in winter.

This palette sits well with rough plaster walls or textured paint effects, such as sponging, that imitate a naturally aged look. For accessories, turn to Mediterranean products, such as glazed wall tiles in deep greens and blues, blue-and-white crockery, terra-cotta pottery, and carved wood.

Furniture might include wrought-iron; mosaic or marble tabletops and countertops; simple, sturdy dark wood; or, if your budget will stretch to it, an eclectic mix of antiques from old Europe.

Opposite: White-painted walls, terra-cotta tiled floors, natural wood, and deep-blue shutters are the staples of the Mediterranean look.

Above: Find inspiration in the colors of citrus fruits, terra-cotta pottery, and the white-and-blue-painted homes of Italy and Greece.

This palette tends toward a relaxed, informal atmosphere, which is ideal for family rooms, dining areas, kitchens, and hallways. Blue plays a central role in nearly any Mediterranean-themed room. Blues can be cooling or surprisingly warm and vibrant. Bringing in the contrast of yellow, red, or terra-cotta creates a perfectly balanced scheme. Flowers and plants are the ideal, simple accessories in any Mediterranean room. They can provide a natural accent color, which will, of course, change with the seasons.

Above: This fresh living room contrasts an electric blue with white-painted tongue-and-groove paneling on the walls and natural wood floors.

Above: Blue and yellow are perfectly balanced in this friendly family kitchen. An antiqued paint effect on the cabinet doors completes the look.

Above: Interest is created in this simple seating area with the use of a vibrant blue, dramatic artwork, and leafy plants.

Above: A Mediterranean feel is created here without the use of blue. A rich burnt sienna harmonizes well with the dark wood and leather upholstery.

Left: Mediterranean-style tiles provide a perfect bath surround, while a sky blue contrasts with white for a fresh feel.

Above: This hallway is made cheerful and welcoming with its mix of orange, bright blue, and white.

Above: The rusts and orange in this living room are lifted by the addition of bright white.

Above: The rough plaster walls are painted a dusty Mediterranean blue, contrasted with pretty pastel pink and lilac.

Above: This veranda teams warm and cool shades for a classic Mediterranean feel: red, pink, and orange on the warm side; blue and white for the cool contrasts.

Above: This welcoming den teams rustic features such as ceiling beams and an open fire with soft, golden yellow and cream.

Color Palette

The Mediterranean palette is very much variations on a simple theme: shades of blue, yellow, and terra-cotta, with off-whites for a little variety. But this palette is enduringly popular, in part because it creates a perfect balance by combining all of the elements: water, air, fire, and earth.

Off-whites

Sky blues

Sea blues

Terra-cottas

Yellows

Oranges

Harmonizing Schemes

The strong colors of the Mediterranean palette need very little embellishment to create a dramatic effect. These simple harmonies, sky with sky and earth with earth, create a focused feel.

Off-whites and pale blue

Sky blues and deep blue

Sea blues and sand

Terra-cotta, red, and orange

Yellow and woody browns

Oranges and lemon

Contrasting Schemes

Contrast is the key to the archetypal Mediterranean look. Mix warm and cool shades—earth and sky—for a perfect balance. Turquoise or bright blue are ideal lifts for rusty browns and terra-cottas, while flat blues can be accented by warm reds and sunshine yellows.

Off-white, deep blue, and orange

Off-white, turquoise, and yellow ocher

Sky blue and sunshine

Sky blue, orange, and oak

Sea blue, turquoise, and orange

Sea blue, deep blue, and sand

Terra-cotta and turquoise

Terra-cotta, deep green, and blue

Yellow, bright blue, and earth

Yellow, pale blue, and aqua

Orange and rich blue

Orange, brown, and turquoise

1 Painting the spice chest the same deep blue as the feature wall gives the room unity. The burnt-orange pillows provide a strong accent.

2 In this option, the traditional shades of terra-cotta, white, and deep blue are refreshingly teamed.

Mediterranean interiors are both informal and inviting, making them ideal for a living area. You can use the Mediterranean palette to alter the perception of a room's proportions, because warm shades such as orange and yellow advance, while cool blues and whites recede. The welcoming living area pictured above combines warm yellow walls with a cream sofa and beige carpet. The dark-wood spice chest completes the look.

3 White walls appear bold, while the rust-colored pillow is an eye-catching contrast to the blue.

4 Sunshine yellow is contrasted with shades of earthy brown, while the blue-painted spice chest provides contrast.

7 Red is an excellent accent color for the sea-blue walls. The practical brown carpet is lightened by the stark white sofa.

5 The terra-cotta floor is balanced by the deep-blue walls. The bright white sofa and sky-blue pillows become the focus.

8 In this scheme, the room appears bigger than it actually is: the white walls lead the eyes upward from the sea-blue carpet.

6 The turquoise woodwork and spice chest, teamed with white walls, create a Greek-island look.

9 The terra-cotta sofa becomes the focus in this cool, pale-blue and white room.

1 Shades of blue always work well together, producing a calm, soothing effect. Here blue is teamed with terra-cotta pillows in a smart white setting.

2 The lower half of the room, with its brown and terra-cotta tones, suggests the earth, while the sky-blue walls lift the eye.

These settings illustrate how powerful white is in Mediterranean schemes. It can either be used as a backdrop, for a cooling, summertime feel, or as a strong accent to the earthy tones of browns, reds, and yellows. In the living area pictured, the tonal and color contrasts of deep blue and white create a bold monochromatic scheme. The feel is bright and inviting.

3 The white flooring and sofa are contrasted with a welcoming terra-cotta, with turquoise accents.

4 This cool scheme of white and shades of blue is cheered by the addition of sunshine-yellow pillows.

5 The orange walls and terra-cotta floor create a welcoming space, with the focus on the white sofa and yellow pillows.

6 Turquoise furniture and white walls and floor create a strong, summertime look.

7 A fuchsia sofa could dominate, but is balanced here by equally strong colors above and below. Again, white unifies the effect.

8 Two shades of blue are twinned with two shades of orange. The effect is balanced and unfussy.

9 White is the base color, enlivened by aqua, yellow, and orange accents.

Exotic Looks

Exotic looks take their inspiration from the color schemes of the tropics, Asia, and the Orient. These schemes can be elegant, playful, or dramatic—but the key is always richness of color combined with luxurious textures in furniture and accessories.

Opposite: This look has the feel of a Middle Eastern palace. Richly hued pillows of lime, saffron, crimson, and purple contrast boldly with the bright gold walls. Textures are silky, and accessories have been chosen for their luxurious feel, giving the room a strong sense of opulence.

A wealth of different color schemes can be described as "exotic," from the subtle shades of Japanese naturals to the rainbow brights of Caribbean colors. In this chapter, you'll find ideas for playing with these different schemes and matching them to soft furnishings and architectural features.

One thing these schemes have in common is their boldness and exuberance. If used without reference to other elements in the room, they could even be a little overpowering. When deciding on an exotic look, the first consideration is whether the style of your room and any existing furnishings match the style you're trying to achieve. A richly detailed living room might suit a Moroccan scheme, while a modern kitchen or dining room might be the ideal home for Mexican brights. But a flamboyant Indian scheme, for example, may not suit a Shaker-style bedroom, unless you would like to play with the shock of contrasts. Whatever scheme you choose, seize the confidence to follow it through in your selection of accessories and furnishings for the room.

A simple Japanese scheme of cream, brown, and indigo would be beautifully matched with the simple, clean lines of Japanese-style furniture and decoration. Avoid pattern and think of texture, in rugs, pillows, and curtains, instead. Accessories should be simple, too, using paper, bamboo, steel, and glass.

In contrast, an Indian scheme of saffron, crimson, and stone would benefit from the dramatic use of detail in accessories and soft furnishings. Think of bold repeating patterns. Mix these with rugs, silks, damasks, and muslins. For accessories, brass, carved wood, tiles, and mirrors would complete the look.

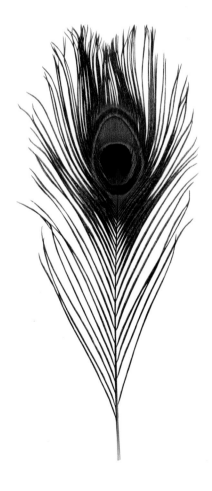

These pictures show a range of the ingredients for exotic-style decor. They feature strong, vibrant colors, often paired with hues of the same intense tonal value. The furnishings are ornate, perhaps intricately carved or luxuriously shaped. The accessories and soft furnishings have been chosen to match the looks: ceramics and carved wood in a Chinese-style room, and marble and metalwork for the Moroccan theme. The feel of all these rooms is welcoming, but also intriguingly complex and opulent.

Above: This hallway evokes a Chinese palace, with its lacquer-effect storage system on the left, clever use of accessories, and the powerful aqua shade of the walls.

Above: An Indian feel has been given to this living room with the use of warm scarlet walls, rich patterns on the sofa and rug, and heavy carved-wood furniture.

Above: This Moroccan-themed living area plays with the strong harmonies of purple, scarlet, and fuchsia. Accessories and furnishings are luxurious.

Above: This bedroom offers a Regency-style take on the Orient, known as Chinoiserie. Bright blue contrasts with gold.

Above: The bathroom is a dramatic place to experiment with exotic decor. The feel of a Middle Eastern palace is supplied by gold walls, marble, and heavy metalwork.

Above: The bold contrast of lilac and dark green create a Caribbean feel in this dramatic bedroom.

Above: Gold is the ideal complement to turquoise in this Southeast Asian-style living room.

Above: The kitchen is the perfect place for a Caribbean scheme. Pineapple is offset by forest green, while the natural stone floor prevents the scheme from being too loud.

 **Above:** Exotic schemes do not have to be costly. Here a Middle Eastern feel is provided by the simple but vibrant contrast of fuchsia and deepest blue.

 **Above:** Red and black are a classic Chinese-style combination, here complemented by dark furniture and accessories.

Mexican

From the boldy painted buildings of the Aztec and Mayan civilizations to the bright-blue and rich-red haciendas of the Spanish colonial period, Mexico has long been alive with color. Mexican colors are fresh, from leaf greens to zingy yellows and citrus oranges. Bright terra-cottas and electric blues are a classic combination, often seen with the muted ochers and reds that remind us of the natural pigments and dyes that were once used. Given the vibrancy of the basic palette, white is a popular accent color.

Rich red with hot orange

Electric blue with hot pink

Indigo with turquoise

Moss green and forest green

Dark blue with sunburnt orange

Off white, bright blue, and red ocher

Persian

Vibrant and bold colors combine with the warm, spicy tones of cinnamon and paprika in this palette. Blue is an essential element of almost any Islamic scheme, used on doors and shutters for the most authentic feel. For a calming look, think of the stones and sands of sunwashed deserts and streets. For a bold style, this palette offers proud, assertive contrasts, such as red with blue, or the opulence of deep blue and purple. For accessories, turn to tiling, ceramics, metalwork, and richly patterned Turkish rugs.

Bright blue, white, and turquoise

Biscuit and mustard

Deep blue, scarlet, and gold

Pale blue, leaf green, and gold

Bright blue and burnt orange

Deep blue, stone, and saffron

Indian

India sparkles with color: the clashing birds-of-paradise shades of saris, the pastel turbans of Rajput princes, the spices of street markets, and the jewel shades of ruby, emerald, sapphire, and topaz. For balance, pair strong colors with others of a similar tone, as with the blood red and bright blue seen below. Colors can also be grouped together in families, such as red, saffron, and orange. When accessorizing, this is one case when less is not more: go for the shine of gold, silver, brass, mirrors, and sequins.

Coral and blues

Saffron, scarlet, and orange

Turquoise and gold

Blood red, bright blue, and white

Red, orange, and olive

Rich purple, navy blue, and lime

Caribbean

When working with this palette, think of tropical fruits: lemons, limes, bananas, pineapples, oranges, or bright-pink pomegranate flesh. These lively colors can be paired with the many shades of the sea, from deep blue to the aquamarines and turquoise of a tropical lagoon. These colors are bright but not bold; gentle and refreshing. A matte texture, such as unvarnished wood, works well with this palette, together with natural materials, such as stone and sisal.

Lime and sea blue

Citrus yellow and burnt orange

Pastel blue and turquoise

Deep green and bright blue

Hot pink and coral pinks

Banana yellow and mossy greens

Chinese

The Chinese palette is made up of intense but clear colors such as a fiery dragon red. The overall style is elaborate yet warm, using rich, vibrant colors that are deeply symobolic to the Chinese themselves. For example, black is a female color, connected with rebirth. Contrasting with this yin is the red male yang of self-expression. Colors are always carefully balanced to create a sense of control and harmony, making this palette particularly suitable for contemporary-style rooms. Off-whites, pearly grays, and gold are common accent colors, while accessories can be lacquer, porcelain, silk, or dark wood.

Black, scarlet, and walnut

Black and gold

Bright blue and silver

Red and gold

Red, dark brown, and purple

Navy blue, yellow, and turquoise

Japanese

This is a palette full of delicate neutrals such as soft gray-greens, creams, and biscuity hues. There is a sense of refinement, balance, and harmony, with great use made of black, white, and grays for subtle contrasts. Strong colors such as red and traditional indigo are restrained by these muted partners. Color schemes tend to be based around a limited set of colors, while complex textures take center stage. Accessorize with delicate fabrics such as linen and silk or organic materials such as stone, paper, and bamboo.

Dark brown and battleship gray

Grays and olive green

Sand and biscuit

Indigo, dove gray, and steel gray

Beige, chocolate, and pale blue

Red, stone, and mahogany

1 This Chinese-style bedroom has a feminine feel. The jade of the walls is an opulent color, teamed here with the warm natural brown of the wood.

2 Here a golden coverlet contrasts with emerald-blue walls for a luxurious Middle Eastern feel.

Using an exotic look in the privacy of the bedroom gives you license to make an extravagant statement. Bedrooms are primarily for rest and relaxation, so team exotic brights with calmer shades for balance. The cozy and feminine bedroom pictured above subtly mixes a Chinese color scheme of gold and wood with an Oriental-style black lacquered cabinet. The opulence and femininity of Eastern color schemes are particularly suited to bedrooms, creating a welcoming, boudoir feel.

3 In this Japanese scheme, gold walls are harmonized with a chocolate coverlet and dark wood.

4 This Moroccan-style bedroom features white walls, a traditional bright-blue door, and a deep-blue coverlet.

7 The pairing of dark-red walls and olive coverlet creates an Indian theme.

5 Red and black are a classic Chinese combination, symbolically pairing male yang and female yin.

8 Black and gold are an archetypal Chinese pairing, offering a pleasing contrast to the intensity of the violet coverlet.

6 This Mexican bedroom contrasts electric blue with hot pink.

9 This Moroccan-style bedroom teams biscuit, emerald, and gold for a luxurious but calm look.

The Chinese calligraphy and Buddha statuette in this living room are perfect accessories for Oriental-style decor. If you own favorite items such as these, it can be worth basing a scheme around them. When using a subtle color palette, artworks can be the focal point of a room. In this scheme, the neutral colors of cream and biscuit draw attention to the symmetry of the styling. Balance is particularly important in Chinese interiors.

1 This bold scheme balances bright dragon red with the black of the furniture. The scheme is lightened by the white carpet.

2 This Japanese scheme of neutral coffee and olive is enlivened by the bold indigo chairs.

5 The stone-colored walls of this Japanese-style room are brought to life by the natural shades of olive green and scarlet in the soft furnishings.

3 Jade walls contrast boldly with the red chair and silver accessories. The balance of colors is important in decorating any room.

6 This neutral but warm palette plays with beige, café au lait, and brown, contrasted with bold Japanese red.

4 Jade and gold is a typical exotic pairing. The neutral bamboo color of the chairs tones it down.

7 The sky blue of the wall is contrasted dramatically with red and gold, for an opulent look.

1 This Mexican palette features the sizzling bold shades of electric blue and hot pink, for a sociable, welcoming room.

2 The fresh shades of banana yellow and lime green are balanced for a Caribbean effect.

These setings illustrate how a dinner set and table decorations can be an integral part of the decor in a dining area. Dining areas are ideal places to play with lively Caribbean colors; the hot, dazzling colors of Mexico; or the opulent hues of the Middle East or India. This simple dining area is given a feel of India simply by the use of a warm paprika on the walls.

3 A rich Indian feel is guaranteed with the use of dark wood, scarlet, and burnt orange.

4 This Islamic-inspired scheme features a trademark blue, contrasted with dark wood for a rich look.

5 The Indian color palette often plays with bold contrasts, such as the clash of saffron, fuchsia, and lime here.

6 This Japanese scheme combines pale grey with the natural shades of indigo and olive.

7 Rust-colored walls complement the browns of the table and chairs and the pairing of olive plates and red napkins for a Moroccan theme.

8 Here a Caribbean coral is teamed with pale wood, creating a soft, convivial atmosphere.

9 Gold is matched with leaf green and accessorized with neutrals and blue for a Middle Eastern look.

Contemporary Living

Contemporary style is all about clean lines, simplicity, and the lack of clutter, allowing space for a house's sculptural elements to shine. Colors are confident and simple, ranging from white and neutrals to unusual brights.

Opposite: White has been used to dramatic and daring effect, leaving a strikingly sculptural chair as the main focus in this loft bedroom.

If you love clean, spare, understated design, this is the style for you. Shades of white are the starting point: brilliant white for the way it accentuates the light in a room together with off-whites, if you'd like to avoid a sterile look. White is the color of peace, freshness, and simplicity, but it also emphasizes light and shadow, so it is the perfect backdrop for architectural details, such as moldings and fireplaces. It also offers space for items of sculptural interest, such as vases, frames, and lamps.

Restricted palettes of neutrals are also the staples of the contemporary look, acting as the perfect backdrop to textures, furniture, or accessories in your scheme. Neutrals are the most practical shades for a family home: they resist stains and match easily with existing elements.

Against this background you can use any strong color. Bright, bold accents will bring zest and vitality. Do not be afraid of black: it defines shapes and spaces. Avoid pastel and cute accent colors. Instead, punch up the room with blocks of unexpected hues, such as turquoise, pea green, or purple. Add textural interest to the paint by having a range of subtle finishes: the softness of matte or the depth of a chalky antiqued-plaster finish.

In the contemporary style, the sleek, pure lines of furniture and architecture are emphasized, so avoid ruffles, pleats, fringes, and tassles. Rather, be bold with soft furnishings such as animal or geometric prints and give them space—imagine how they might be displayed in a museum. Consider using a range of textures: the pile of a rug, the weave of a linen curtain, or the softness of wool, silk, or jute. Glass, metal, stone, and even plastic accessories will complete the look.

In these rooms, bold flat color is combined with interesting architectural features, such as a modern fireplace or spiral staircase. The clean, clear lines of functional design are allowed to shine. Carefully chosen accessories—a dramatic light fixture or a giant vase, take center stage. Contemporary living is not just about style, however: it's also about comfort and useability, so opt for colors that are ideal for the space and function of the room—white to lighten a space, deep blue to resist stains in a kitchen, bright chairs in a dining room to welcome guests.

Above: Black has been used here to define this unusual space. Flowers both accentuate and soften the lines of contemporary decor.

Above: In this white-painted dining area, the eye is drawn to the boldly colored chairs, underlining the function of the room.

Above: This welcoming chair adds interest to an otherwise neutral scheme of white and natural wood.

Above: The color scheme of this kitchen is so subtle you barely notice it is there. Black and white tiling, white-painted walls, dark wood, and steel create a sophisticated feel.

Above: Line can be the most important element in a contemporary interior, as with this beautifully proportioned fireplace. Natural materials such as pebbles and the wood floor offer contrast to the ice-blue walls.

Left: This kitchen demonstrates the dramatic effect of a well-chosen but surprising shade. The opulent blue links wonderfully with the burnt orange of the next room.

Above: Contemporary style doesn't have to be unwelcoming. This living room teams unusual coral walls with a fuchsia sofa and chunky furniture.

Above: The unexpected clash of fuchsia and bright yellow in the soft furnishings is teamed with stark white walls.

Above: Gray is underrated as a color for decoration: when teamed with brights, such as the blue, pink, and lime pillows, here, it can create a smart and vibrant ambiance.

Above: A bold purple is teamed with pale wood and metal for a thoroughly modern dining area.

Above: Contemporary styling exploits architectural features such as this stairway. White and gray provide the ideal backdrop.

Above: In this white open-plan living area, the unusual seating feels welcoming because of its soft curves and the warm, rich reds and blues of the fabrics.

Above: Shades of blue are a classic contemporary choice, but the romantic, extravagant lilacs and mauve are essential to keep this bedroom feeling feminine.

Above: Gray and white are a dramatic pairing. Stark, metal-legged furniture completes the look.

Above: A clever combination of blues and greens keeps the scheme natural while accentuating the many different shapes and lines in this pretty kitchen.

Right: Mottled dark gray creates a mature backdrop, where the curvilinear sofa, sculpture, and painting can shine.

Color Palette

The contemporary palette contains many neutral colors as well as strikingly bold hues. Note that each color is a little surprising in its shade: a green that veers toward pea, a burgundy edging toward brown, a gray that seems blue in one light and black in another. When using contemporary colors on their own, consider adding a subtle texture for interest.

Off-whites

Biscuits

Grays

Creams

Yellows

Turquoises

Greens

Burgundies

Purples

Reds

Pinks

Rich blues

Harmonizing Schemes

It is worth experimenting with the proportions of these harmonizing schemes. Used in equal measures, the colors will create a striking balance. Alternatively, it is common to create a neutral backdrop, then just add a splash of a bright, demanding shade as accent in contemporary schemes.

Off-whites and brown

Biscuits and olive

Grays and royal blue

Cream and blues

Yellow and walnut

Turquoises and navy

Green, brown, and cream

Burgundy and pink

Purples and warm pink

Reds and cream

Pink and chocolate

Rich blues and sky blue

Contrasting Schemes

Be prepared to make bold statements with this palette. The neutral canvas so common in contemporary decor can be spiced up with a splash of several contrasting shades in soft furnishings or accessories. For an audacious look, consider painting one or two feature walls in contrasting colors.

Off-whites and black

Biscuit, deep blue, and scarlet

Gray, pink, and yellow

Cream, brown, and lime

Yellow and lilacs

Turquoise and pink

Green and red

Burgundy and green

Purples and orange

Red, black, and orange

Pink and pea green

Deep blue and pink

The living room is a great place to use the contemporary palette. Modern neutrals are practical, hard-wearing colors, while splashes of contemporary brights can add interest, warmth, and vitality to the room. Pillows offer an excellent opportunity for playing with bold accents. The room pictured above has classic contemporary styling, with a restricted, understated neutral palette. Simple but confident accessories complete the look.

1 Painting one wall a rich deep blue is bold, but the eye is also drawn to the lime-green cushions, retaining a balance in visual interest.

2 Gray walls are made warm and welcoming by the cozy royal blue of the sofa.

3 Red and black is a striking, vibrant combination set against a backdrop of pale neutral shades.

6 Yellow and pale blue are a pleasing combination. The sunshine-yellow feature wall draws the eye to the fireplace.

4 This striking combination of neutrals, black, and white creates a mature, confident statement.

7 The silver and gold pillows create an opulent focus in this sophisticated white, black, and gray setting.

5 This bold, masculine room makes dramatic use of a white canvas, enlivened by bold color accents.

8 Royal blue is contrasted with warm shades of red-brown for a strong, modern look.

We like our bedrooms to be calm but not clinical, so it is important to include relaxing colors and interesting textures. The large window in this bedroom floods the room with light, which can be softened by delicate soft fabrics. These strong shades of pink and blue create a lively contrast, punctuated by a surprising shot of lemon.

1 This classic monochromatic scheme of white and blue is given added complexity by the green and yellow pillows.

2 Pillows in red and lilac plus a cherry-red coverlet maintain visual interest in front of the beige walls.

3 The neutral floor and curtains act as a backdrop for the bold bedding and orange feature wall.

4 This masculine color scheme has entirely changed the feel of the bedroom. The navy, gray, and black are given a bright accent by the luminous yellow.

7 Against a neutral backdrop of brown and mushroom, the clash of the bright purple feature wall and leaf-green coverlet create a bold focus.

5 This is a bold scheme of surprising contrasts. The dark-pink feature wall is set off by the white canvas of the other walls.

8 Shades of blue and purple are teamed with cooler neutrals, drawing attention to the bed area.

6 A feminine scheme of turquoise, blue, and lilac is teamed with neutrals.

9 Pale neutrals of cream and wood are lifted by the addition of emerald and sapphire soft furnishings.

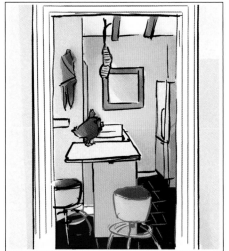

1 The bold contrast of red and black is softened by the inclusion of the midway tints of gray and peach.

2 This would be a simple Mediterranean scheme of terra-cotta and blue, without the twist of the lime-green stools.

Painting different walls in contrasting shades is a popular contemporary effect that creates interest and depth. This modern kitchen, with its clean, bold lines, is a good canvas for playing with this style. Flat matte panels of lilac, green, and terra-cotta have been teamed for a warm contemporary appearance.

3 Olive and mint-green walls contrast refreshingly with the bold purple stools.

4 Shades of yellow on the walls offer tonal contrast with the black floor, while the royal-blue counter provides color contrast.

5 A warm family of colors—terra-cotta, orange, and yellow—is teamed with a calming off-white wall.

6 A checkerboard floor gives structure to this neutral scheme, while red stools provide accent.

7 Pink and red are unusual and daring colors to choose for a kitchen. Here they're set against a classic neutral backdrop.

8 This refreshing room is fixed firmly in neutrals, with the subtle contrast of coral and dusty-lime walls.

9 Purple and orange are teamed for a sizzling contrast, while neutrals provide a framework.

Period Colors

Using period colors in your period-built home creates a link with history and a strong sense of place. But using carefully chosen period shades in a modern home can create a whole new feeling of identity and depth.

Opposite: This lovely nineteenth-century home uses the Victorian shades of burgundy and dusty peach-pink in adjoining rooms. Soft furnishings are in Arts and Crafts florals and heavy harmonizing velvets.

Many homeowners like to match the decor of their home to the era in which it was built in order to make the most of its architectural style. If, however, like most homeowners, your house is modern in style, period colors can still add interest to your home. A gothic hallway, for example, is a statement that your house is stimulating and unique.

The increasing interest in period colors is reflected in the ranges of historic paints manufacturers are now producing. These modern paints are an approximation of historic shades, because today chemicals replace natural pigments and dyes for ease of application and stability of color. Try browsing your local stores and picking up palettes and samples to get an idea of what is available.

In this chapter, you will find an overview of color trends from the ancient Greeks to the minimalist 1990s, with particular reference to the past two hundred years. In the last century, tastes in decor have changed as quickly as tastes in clothes. You may feel certain that, just as you wouldn't wear a flapper dress or flairs, you wouldn't choose dull Bauhaus colors or the acid hues of the 1970s—but think again. Even if you decide against a whole room in these colors, period palettes can provide vital inspiration for the twenty-first-century decorator.

Paint techniques can work exceptionally well with period schemes, whether it's a trompe l'oeil mural for a medieval look or sponging for a postmodern 1980s scheme. Consider your accessories and furnishings carefully. An Art Deco color scheme, for example, may just look placidly pastel if not combined with geometrically patterned soft furnishings and 1920s-style vases and lamps.

If your home has outstanding architectural or decorative features, you probably want to make the most of them. A good idea is to paint them in the colors that were originally used when they were created, so that they look just as they were intended. Or you might feel that your furniture has wonderful baroque curves, or a Shaker simplicity, so why not try out colors from the relevant period and explore the effect? The rooms shown here offer a mixture of genuine period detail and imaginative use of period colors. If you like the results, it works!

Above: This simple room with wooden detailing makes perfect use of the Shaker palette. Shaker schemes generally feature flat, matte greens, navies, and burgundies against a cream ground.

Above: This bedroom is in classic 1980s style: masculine, structured, and confident.

Above: The golds, stones, and rich browns of this room are borrowed from the ancient Roman palette. The feel is opulent but natural, like an imperial provincial villa.

Left: This handsomely detailed room uses the American Colonial palette: dull red and forest green teamed with a cream canvas.

Below: The Georgian pink on the walls is complemented by a fine carpet and toning scarves at the window.

Above: This very simple scheme of unpainted wood floorboards with cream and green woodwork brings to mind middle-class American Colonial style of the eighteenth century.

Below: This simply elegant room uses the colors of Swedish neoclassical style: a simple dull green against a white canvas.

Below: The bold colors and plastic surfaces of a 1950s diner are perfect for this neat little breakfast area. The look is completed by the car artworks on the walls.

Left: Green was an extremely popular color for decoration in Georgian England. Here it is combined with the neutrally painted wood paneling of an early eighteenth-century English home.

Above: Gold was central to the Rococo palette. Here it is combined with claret in this grand and luxurious bedroom.

Left: Italian neoclassical style of the late eighteenth century made subtle use of soft neutrals, combined with heavy furniture, rich fabrics, and golden accessories.

Color Palette

Early paints were pigment based, and so tended toward earthiness, like the terra-cotta of ancient Greek and Roman times. After the Renaissance, when pigment production came under the control of guilds of colorists, the use of color in decoration became increasingly sophisticated. Each era had a favorite hue, such as the greens of the Georgians and the purples of baroque.

Ancient Greek

Terra-cotta and soot black

Bright blue, red ocher, and stone

Gold, flesh, and clay

Stone, brown, and red

Ancient Roman

Sand, rust, and blue-gray

Gold, scarlet, and gray

Medieval

Woad blue, cream, and gold

Purple-red, stone, and rust

Crimson, saturated green, and gold

Burgundy, clove pink, and silver

Yellow, weld brown, and madder red

Deep blue, turquoise, and brown

European Baroque 1600–1750

Purple and yellow ocher

Indigo and deep blues

Red and gold

Dark green, brown, and gold

English Georgian 1714–1760

Pea green, pinkish stone, and brown

Deep green, burgundy, and oak

American Colonial 1640–1776

Cool blue and wood

Fleet blue and cream

Deep green, forest green, and cream

Red-pink and stones

American Neoclassical 1750–1850

Gray-green, oak, and white

Scarlet, yellow-green, and cream

French Rococo 1725–1780

Pastel pink and white

Gold and sage

Pale blue and lilac

Pale pink, gray, and cream

Shaker 1750–1900

Soldier blue, cream, and wood

Dull red, cream, and biscuit

Victorian 1837–1901

Sunshine yellow and forest green

Powder blue, beige, and Chinese red

Arts and Crafts 1860–1910

Cream, terra-cotta, and mustard yellow

Olive green and walnut

Forest green and biscuit

Dusty blue, brown, and rust

Art Nouveau 1880–1910

Mustard, orange, and brown

Olive green, brown, and cream

Off-white, violet, and purple

Dark olive, cream, and rose

Art Deco 1908–1930s

Pale pinks and mint

Orange, lime, and lemon

Bauhaus 1919–1930s

Red, yellow, and blue

Black, red, and cream

1940s

Beige and dusty rose

Cherry red and straw

Moss green and yellows

Soft blue and fuchsia pink

1950s

Pastel pink, red, and dark cream

Aquamarine and kingfisher blue

Washed lime, dark pink, and yellow

Turquoise, off-white, and black

Rose pink and pastel pinks

Vanilla, pink, and mint

1960s

Bright red, dark blue, and biscuit

Hot pink, red, and bright blue

Orange, red, and purple

Black and off-whites

Tangerine and fuchsia pink

Violet, sage green, and washed orange

1970s

Avocado, straw, and yellow

Harvest gold with olives

Orange, red, and bright yellow

Bright yellow and browns

Lime green, hot orange, and beige

Browns and dark pink

1980s

Midnight blue, bright red, and beige

Ash gray, Reagan red, and burgundy

Chrome gray, silver, and beige

Black and red

1990s

Tobacco, lion's mane, and navy

Indigo and wheat

This traditionally furnished bedroom is well suited to pre-twentieth-century palettes, such as Victorian, Georgian, and American Colonial. Its scheme of burgundy, dark green, and a floral-patterned coverlet is characteristic of the Arts and Crafts movement—the style pioneered by Britain's William Morris. However, the feel of the room can be dramatically changed by the use of a surprising color scheme, such as 1960s luminous brights or Art Deco pastels.

1 This Victorian color scheme combines burgundy and dull forest green.

2 A warm pink contrasts with the cool of the powder-blue walls in this 1940s-style look.

3 The simple, flat colors of American Colonial style have been used here: cream, navy, and forest green.

6 Cool Georgian creams and blue make the bedroom feel classic and airy.

4 These vivid 1960s colors are fun and confident. The patterned coverlet completes the effect.

7 This Victorian palette of dusty rose and dark green matches the heavy wood furniture perfectly.

5 This Art Deco scheme makes use of the sweet pastels of pink, lilac, and lemon.

8 This subtle look uses the delicate shades of French Rococo, lightening the effect of the dark furniture.

Choosing period colors is a very personal choice, and you can select any era if the end result works for you. This is a Victorian bathroom, so schemes that work best are generally nineteenth century, but the use of a sensitive 1970s or medieval color scheme can also create a sympathetic effect. The Victorian features of this bathroom are left to speak for themselves with the unobtrusive but authentic scheme of cream, white, and marble pictured above.

1 These rich shades of brown and green create an alternative Victorian scheme.

2 This warm orange is typical of Art Nouveau interiors. It creates a coziness in an otherwise quite stark interior.

3 The avocado, cream, and brown of the 1970s style create a comfortable, unpretentious look.

6 Green-painted wood paneling was the signature look in the Georgian period. Here the scheme is given a lift by the gold-upholstered chair.

4 Pale gray and dark pink are medieval colors, here lifted by the golden orange chair. The scheme creates a pretty, inviting space.

7 Dark-brown wood paneling combined with sky blue and green create a nature-inspired Art Nouveau feel.

5 The soldier-blue paneling teamed with cream walls is an essential element of the Shaker style.

8 This British Edwardian look teams an olive bath with shades of green and brown.

Enhancing Your Space

If your room is too dark, too light, too small, too large, too tall, or too narrow, careful color choices can correct the balance. The key thing to bear in mind is that dark or warm hues seem to advance toward us, while lighter, cooler colors appear to recede.

Opposite: White is the ultimate space-creator, here making the floor and doors recede, thus widening this narrow corridor. Lighting can also dramatically change how we perceive space—here the uplight floods the ceiling with light, lifting the eyes and making the space seem less cramped.

Light colors reflect more light, making them appear to be further away, so they are ideal for making small rooms or areas seem larger. Dark colors have the opposite effect and can be used to draw in parts of a room.

We can play with these effects to disguise awkward proportions. For example, by painting a ceiling and the trim below it the same color, it can be made to seem lower. Painting a ceiling a bright white is a common means of creating the sense of a higher ceiling. Similarly, dark floors will draw the eye downward. Painting them lighter and cooler focuses our attention higher, making the room seem taller.

As we make more demands on the different spaces in our homes—using part of a room as an office or media zone, or opting for informal dining areas rather than having a room dedicated to eating—colors can help to define these areas, making them separate but part of the whole. For example, using a different but harmonizing color on a feature wall behind a dining area will visually separate it from an adjacent seating area without creating a jarring scheme.

Color can also be used to change the light and mood in a room. In a dark room that receives little natural light, try sunny tones such as yellows, golds, pinks, and reds. Colors in the warm and cozy palette (see pages 48–63) can make a large or featureless room feel welcoming. Cool colors such as pale blues and greens will create a restful feeling of light and space. Deep red is hot and passionate, stimulating the senses, and is ideal for dining areas.

Experiment with using colors to focus the eye on different areas in the room, such as a welcoming red sofa or bed coverlet, or on a favorite artwork on a feature wall.

Successful decorating is all about the balance between hot and cold colors, where the eye is to be drawn, and the balance between flat expanses and textured detail. The following photographs highlight how colors, details, and textures can be used to create a sense of harmony and balance in even the most awkward spaces. Even if you are blessed with a pleasingly proportioned home, consider how color can be used to make the most of your natural features and evoke a mood.

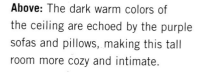

Above: This small bedroom looks airy painted a space-enhancing pale blue. This color creates a contemplative feel, ideal for a restful, private area.

Above: The dark warm colors of the ceiling are echoed by the purple sofas and pillows, making this tall room more cozy and intimate.

Above: A translucent fabric blind softens the light entering through the expansive windows, while the dark floor prevents the dramatic space from feeling clinical.

Left: In this small and potentially claustrophobic space, pale neutrals and white are used to give a feeling of space. The ceiling is also kept white to open up the room.

Left: For warmth, oranges, reds, and browns are an ideal combination. A common technique for creating depth or differentiating areas in a room is to paint walls in different colors. Here brown and peach colors appear on adjoining walls.

Above: This kitchen is narrow, so the side walls have been painted in black, which appears to recede, while the eye is drawn to the white end wall.

Left: There is so much architectural interest here from the paneling and molding that all this entryway needs is a white backdrop to reflect light into every corner.

Above: The different areas of this long, narrow living area are differentiated by the blue ceiling beam. Interest and depth are created by painting the alcoves in a darker, receding blue.

Above: This kitchen is full of fascinating lines and planes. Attention is drawn to the sloping ceiling by painting it a dusty blue, while the rest of the kitchen area is differentiated by a rich China blue.

Above: Dark corners are cold and uninviting, restricting the space we want to use. Here a strategically placed downlight and a blend of warm oranges and white keeps the hallway welcoming.

Creating Space

Off-whites

Pale creams

Pale blues

Pale greens

Pale wheats

Pale turquoises

Creating Light

Lilacs

Pinks

Yellows

Oranges

Creating Warmth

Reds

Purples

This study area is a tricky space. The corridor is narrow, and there is a lack of natural light, which could make the corner appear dark and uninviting. Painting the ceiling white prevents the area from feeling claustrophobic. The pale blues are restful, while creating a feeling of light and space. The stripe running through the decoration leads the eye ahead and adds interest to an otherwise featureless room.

1 White is the ideal color for creating light and space. The turquoise stripe provides interest.

2 This sunny cream creates a sense of sunlight. The leaf-green carpet creates a natural scheme.

3 As cool colors, these shades of turquoise recede, enhancing the space.

4 Putting the most attention-seeking color on the blind draws the eye. The sunny yellow creates a cheery look.

7 This sunny scheme draws the eye upward from the dark floor to the white upper walls and ceiling.

5 Darker lower walls and lighter harmonizing upper walls and ceiling are ideal for preventing the space from feeling enclosed.

8 Cream, saffron, and brown create a light and bright scheme.

6 Pale greens and blues create a contemplative and restful scheme.

9 This neutral scheme is lifted by the bold stripe of purple, drawing the eye to the end of the room.

1 The choice of a contemporary turquoise creates a dramatic modern space. The eye is drawn upward from the dark floor to the lighter ceiling.

2 A warm orange creates a welcoming entryway. The dark floor and light ceiling create a sense of space.

3 This bold, modern look makes the area seem smaller without closing it in from above.

This dramatic entryway is full of interesting lines and shapes. The question is whether to create a scheme that unifies the whole space or to draw attention to the different areas and features. Depending on the color scheme, this space could be grand and dramatic or warm and cozy. In the photo above, the creams and neutrals create a classic, elegant look.

4 The white floor and walls make the area seem huge, while the darker ceiling focuses attention on its interesting shapes.

5 This is a dramatic look, creating a bold exciting space delineated by the black stairway.

6 Pink makes the space cozier and sunnier, while the white ceiling creates airiness.

7 The cream floor coupled with darker walls leads the eye through the area toward the adjoining rooms.

8 This Mediterranean scheme of terra-cotta, pale blue, and white is ideal for creating sunlit space.

9 Pale greens reflect light and open up the space, while the darker floor grounds the room.

In this tiny bedroom, it's important to create space and depth. Paler colors will suggest space, while adding contrast through the use of contrasting colors on different walls will create depth. Here the sunny shades of red and yellow prevent the room from feeling dark. The sloping ceiling is painted the same color as the wall to prevent the bedroom from feeling enclosed.

1 The use of white will always create space. The effect is prevented from becoming sterile by the addition of a bold blue coverlet.

2 Neutrals make the most of the space, while the burgundy door creates interest and accent.

3 Pale blue always creates light and space, while the darker blue in the recess suggests depth.

4 Pale green reflects light and suggests space, while the red of the coverlet creates accent.

5 This Mediterranean scheme suggests sunshine. The pale walls and ceiling create space.

6 This Moroccan-style look creates both space and interest.

7 If you want to make the most of the light but aren't keen on neutral schemes, go for a variety of yellows that will keep the effect airy but welcoming.

8 This dramatic Chinese-style scheme creates both light and depth with the use of the contrasting white and red.

9 This pale pink exudes light and color, while the green coverlet prevents the look being oversweet.

The striking bath is a pleasing shape but can all too easily dominate this small room. Another problem is the off-center window which leaves one corner looking dark and neglected. The wooden paneling is a great natural feature that can be used to provide interest and focus.

1 A cool refreshing green reinforces the outlines of the bath in front of it. Pale blue walls add height.

2 A darker color on the top half of the room draws attention to the interesting sloping ceiling.

3 Purple is always a bold choice for decoration: here it is ideal for creating interest and color.

6 Warm red, pink, and cream create an inviting space. The black enameling of the bath creates a strong contrast.

4 Creating in effect three bands of color across the room stretches it so that it seems wider, while the hues have a warm, cozy feel.

7 A cooler, refreshing effect is created with space-enhancing soft green and blue.

5 These sunny tones create a light feel, while the bolder tone on the upper wall lifts the eye upward.

8 White has created a sense of space, while the bold blue makes a feature of the sloping ceiling.

This is a small, rather cluttered space with the dining table edging up to the fireplace. The key here is to exploit contrasts and layers to emphasize what depth there is. The bright blue and hot pink make a sizzling contrast, creating focus and drama.

1 The use of restful browns and creams unifies the space, while the painting of one wall a paler shade creates space and delineates the dining area.

2 The bold, energizing red creates a series of stripes, making the room seem taller.

3 This rich brown creates a cozy space, while the eye is drawn to the paler fireplace.

4 The pale blue is airy and creates space, while the darker blue recedes, suggesting depth.

7 The darker brown in the alcoves creates depth in this subtle and restful neutral scheme.

5 Sunny yellow lightens this dark room; the dark floor and paler ceiling draw the eye upward.

8 The focus in this room is clearly on the bright and welcoming fireplace wall.

6 This rich Victorian scheme creates a cozy space, while the hearth remains the focus.

9 The darker green in the alcoves creates a sense of layers, making the most of the cramped space.

1 A range of cool, airy blue-greens makes the space soothing but interesting. Matching the ceiling to the inner drape keeps the space unified.

2 The harmonizing pinks create a suggestion of sunlight in the dark space. The paler pink on the upper wall draws the eye upward.

3 Darkening the floor and lower wall lifts the eye to open up the space.

Small, tight spaces appear bigger when they are bathed in light, which can be achieved through large mirrors, as in this bedroom. In a tiny room, the question is whether to create space by the use of one pale, uniform color or to create depth by using blocks of contrasting colors. The contrast of orange and purple in the draperies and coverlet creates interest and focus in what could be a featureless room.

4 Neutrals expand space, and there are enough contrasts here to avoid the trap of becoming too bland and uniform.

7 Adjoining walls in contrasting gray and peach create interest, while the eye is lifted above the dark-gray carpet.

5 The orange feature wall gives depth, while the pale, sunny shades imply greater space and light.

8 This cozy scheme makes good use of a pale cream on the far wall to suggest space and air.

6 A warm, pale yellow opens up the room and bathes it in light.

9 This contemplative natural scheme of green and pale gold creates a restful feel.

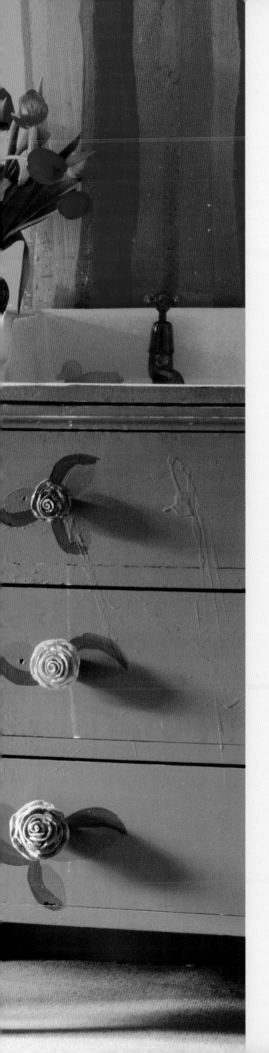

Choosing Paint Techniques

There is an amazing range of paint techniques from which to choose. Techniques can add interest, depth, or drama to painted areas. In the "Making Pictures" chapter, choose between bold designs such as murals and patterns or pick out a border to complete a look. The "Textural Finishes" chapter offers ideas for adding rhythm to your painted surfaces through techniques such as ragging or sponging. And finally, the "Faux Techniques" chapter is a catalog of effects that mimic the look of materials such as fabrics, metals, wood, or stone.

Making Pictures

Adding patterns, borders, or scenes to a painted wall, creates a highly individual look. Inspiration for these techniques can be found in period decoration, from the wallpaintings of ancient Greece to the frescoes of Renaissance Florence.

Opposite: Shades of lilac and purple form a textured, geometric backdrop to add interest to this pretty bedroom. The pale color scheme prevents the checks from becoming overpowering, while the white-painted floor creates a sense of space.

Sometimes you may feel that plain blocks of color will be overly uniform or dull. Choosing to add pattern or pictures will create interest. Using wallpaper is an option, of course, but using paint gives you the chance to bring a genuinely unique look to a room—unless you have a large budget and can invest in custom-made wallpaper. Using paint gives you control and flexibility, and can be less expensive than wallpaper if you undertake the decoration yourself. If doing the job yourself, practice on card or a small area first. Unless you are a confident artist and can paint freehand, try experimenting with photocopies, projected images, and stencils.

Patterns can be visually and texturally stimulating. Your look can be subtle, with faint stripes or fleur-de-lys, or vibrant, with checks or geometric designs.

Consider the size of your room and the effect you hope to achieve. For example, vertical stripes make a room seem taller, while large patterns close in the space. Patterned borders can be used to define the spaces in a room.

There is a long tradition of adding pictures to walls and floors, from the very earliest hunting scenes on the walls of caves to the sophisticated frescoes of fifteenth-century Europe. If you are looking for a way to add period character to a room, well-chosen frescoes will transport it back several hundred years.

Alternatively, try a playful look by painting Venetian Baroque cherubs on your dining room walls. For real drama, trompe l'oeil is the answer. This technique can give an extraordinary impression of three dimensional space, adding depth and creating variety in your home.

Children's Rooms

Children's rooms are a great place to make pictures. Involve your children as much as possible. They are much more likely to look after their rooms if they know how much effort the scheme took to create. Children enjoy playing with ideas, so it should be easy to agree on a color scheme and a theme. The tricky thing might be carrying out that theme. If you are using professionals to do the job, tell them your theme, such as the circus or the zoo, and ask them to come up with designs and variations. If you're undertaking the job yourself, choose a technique with which you are comfortable—such as stenciling or stamping—and base your scheme around that. Don't worry if you are not brilliant at art: being bright and playful are the key ideas here. For example, you could use a repeating pattern of your child's handprints, which will also be lots of fun to create. This is your chance to be bold. When the children become tired with their rooms, they should be old enough to make changes themselves!

Tree motifs stenciled in various shades of green make a restful and cheery nursery.

These hand-drawn ribbons of paint flowing from tubes make a rainbow effect, and the wobbles just add to their charm.

In this teenager's room, a stenciled moon sits under a stylized sun and star design. The curves of the decorative ribbons soften the hard lines.

Flowers hand-painted onto the wall echo the patterns on the coverlet and bedhead.

If there is a drawing you'd like to include, such as this goose, try tracing it.

Clouds sponged onto the ceiling, teamed with blue-striped cabinets and bright-pink walls, create a fun and playful nursery.

One advantage of stencils is that you can change their orientation as you work, as illustrated in this pretty bedroom.

Borders

Borders shift the visual focus, changing the perceived proportions of a room. This can be handy if you want to make a ceiling seem lower, for example. Borders also help to define a space and create fresh interest. The idea came to the Americas from Europe in the eighteenth century, when borders started to appear in colonial living rooms. At this time, border designs were kept classically simple. Their style should always match that of the room. For example, hand-drawn borders will blend with an Indian- or Mexican-themed interior very well. Borders can be placed at chair- or picture-rail height, and work best when they are run all around a room, creating a unified effect. Wood- or stone-effect borders are another option for introducing a new texture to a room. Borders are also fine vehicles for bringing an accent color to all sides of a room. Complex patterns can be stenciled, or trace designs from wallpaper, wrapping paper, or art books.

This gray-green crown molding matches the dark furniture in the room and forms a helpful barrier between the yellow of the walls and the green of the ceiling, which would otherwise jar at their meeting point.

This striped border of orange and gray links the orange of the wall with the light-gray furnishings, helping to unify the look of the room. The geometric pattern also echoes the shapes of the painting.

A stenciled lily defines the corner of the room, while a leaf motif has been applied around the edge of the floor.

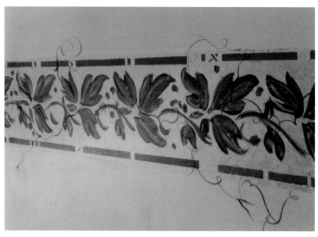

This Florentine-style floral border, with its palette of terracotta and green, creates a period look.

This pretty blue and gold border lowers the perceived height of the ceiling.

Borders can feature words as well as pictures. These stencils emphasize the importance of the wine store.

Frescoes

Artists have been painting pictures on walls for millennia. The technique known as fresco painting was developed in medieval Italy and perfected during the Renaissance period. Literally, frescoes are pictures on walls or ceilings that are painted by applying colors to plaster that is still fresh (fresco means "fresh" in Italian). But today modern paints can be applied to dry plaster. The technique can transform a room, literally taking it into another dimension. Popular fresco looks hark back to period designs, such as fanciful Rococo scenes or 1960s pop art murals. Unless you are a confident artist, you will probably find frescoes a little daunting to undertake yourself. You could try experimenting with applied photocopied images or by projecting slide images onto your wall and then tracing them. Alternatively, employ a professional decorator who has a portfolio of scenes in the style and budget that suit your needs.

Painted clouds on a ceiling is a neoclassical effect that creates a feeling of light and space.

This magical unending pathway creates an illusion of extra space on this stairway.

A cartoon-style fresco featuring caricatures of chefs and waiters creates a talking point in this kitchen.

This airy neoclassical vista, complete with columns and temples, opens up this small kitchen and dining area.

A pastoral scene over the fireplace lifts this room. The creams and greens used in the picture match the shades of the rug and furniture. Whatever your choice of technique, the color choices should still be part of your overall decorative plan.

What could be an uninviting windowless space is transformed into a "verdant garden" with this Florentine-style fresco in natural terra-cottas and greens on plaster-colored walls.

Patterns

Patterns add flair and individuality to a decorative scheme. They are an ideal vehicle for introducing accent colors, and a good way of breaking up blocks of solid color. Start by choosing the colors for the pattern, taking them from your main color scheme. Patterns, such as the simple repeating motifs seen in Greek villas, have been used to add interest to walls and floors since ancient times. In the twentieth century, bold geometric patterns became the trademark of the Art Deco style. Your choice of pattern can be decided partly by the proportions of the room: big shapes will be fine in large rooms but will dominate small rooms, and small checks or spots will be lost in a large room. If you opt for two styles, vary their sizes. For example, put a large grid behind a smaller floral motif, but maintain unity by using similar colors for each. Try using vertical stripes to make a room appear taller, and busy patterns to make a space more intimate.

The style of the patterns on both the walls and floor are of a Matisse-inspired cut-out.

Repeating patterns allows you to play with varying colors and backgrounds while retaining a unified look.

Painting on dots is a simple technique that adds texture to flat color.

These subtle wide stripes in neutral gray create a clean, sophisticated effect.

Hand-drawing basic patterns creates a simple rustic charm. You can add artistic flourishes like this flower.

Painting vertical and horizontal lines freehand creates a check pattern to match the gingham curtain.

The grid on this kitchen floor is painted in beige to suggest tiles, while the lines are softened by the repeating pattern. A top coat of varnish seals the finish.

Abstract shapes in a limited palette of colors produces a strikingly individual powder room.

Dotted gold lines create a modern paneled effect that is an intriguing backdrop for frames.

This bold modern look has been created by teaming delicately striped walls with a multicolored sideboard.

Using a limited palette of neutral colors produces a refined, elegant effect here. The top half of the wall has been painted in subtly contrasting cream-and-tan stripes, echoing the colors and pattern of the wooden floor. A slightly deeper shade below the chair rail stops the look from becoming too fussy. White is a perfect accent color for this classical style.

Painting rather than papering allows you to find a perfect match for a color already present in the room. Here broad horizontal bands widen the appearance of a small bathroom, while repeating the colors in the backsplash and its partner picture. The mounted patterned picture matches the colors and motifs of the tiles to finish a simple, creative scheme.

Stamps and Stencils

Stenciling and stamping are fantastic for adding repeating patterns and making a room look truly individual in an inexpensive and simple way. Stencils have been used in China since about 3000 B.C., when they were applied to silks and paper. The technique was also employed extensively in Regency interiors, and was very popular in Victorian decor. For example, leading Arts and Crafts designer William Morris used stencils widely. The method is simple: paint is applied through a cutout made from thick card or acetate, giving the impression of hand-painting. Stenciling allows repeated use of identical shapes that can be set at regular intervals or in groups, or rotated to introduce an element of surprise. For corners and curves, use acetate for your template, although the sheets can be slippery. You can make your own stencils or buy them ready-cut. Rubber stamps are used in a similar way, and many craft shops will be able to prepare a stamp in your motif.

Flooring is a great place to use stencils, such as this simple flower design. Varnish it after the paint dries.

Delicate white feathers have been stenciled onto the lilac walls of this feminine bedroom.

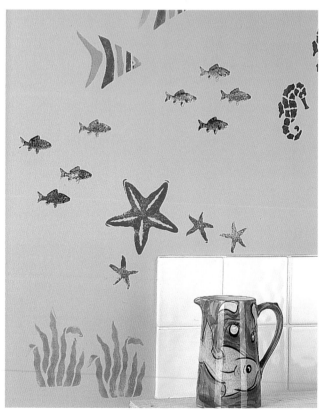

Homemade stamps have been used to create an underwater-themed bathroom.

This clever use of stencils creates the impression of a stair carpet. It needs to be well sealed for protection.

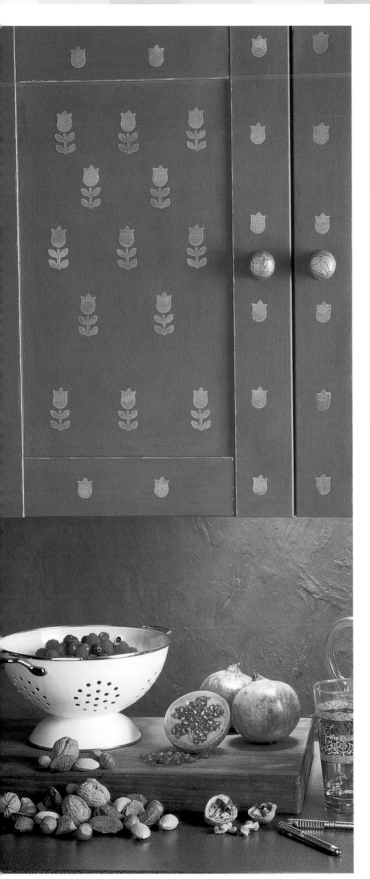

Stamping is the ideal way to reproduce complicated shapes, such as these ascending treble clefs.

A simple flower design has been stamped onto a claret cabinet for a medieval-style look.

Stencils allow you to use more than one color for a truly hand-painted effect.

Trompe l'Oeil

Trompe l'oeil means "trick the eye" in French and is a painting technique that allows you to give the impression of three-dimensional space, such as a view through a window. The ancient Romans employed this method to bring a feeling of light and space to dark interiors, and it is part of the armory of the classical style of decoration. In the grand houses of eighteenth-century Europe, it was fashionable to add fake arches and trelliswork to interior walls. Trompe l'oeil was also employed to conjure up architectural features, such as columns and moldings. The dramatic effects of trompe l'oeil can work well in both small and large spaces—creating drama in a large entryway or preventing a feeling of enclosure in a small powder room. The technique requires good drawing skills for its subtle manipulation of light and shade, but projecting an image onto a wall and tracing it is one way to reproduce an effect without relying on your own sense of scale and proportion.

The narrow corridor from this room has been given fake stonework and a space-inducing arched recess.

This Parisian street scene transforms a blank wall into a dramatic stage set.

Beautifully proportioned earthenware vases and a stylish marble basin perfectly complement the faux window surround and marble-effect walls in this bathroom. Trompe l'oeil is especially well suited to classical-style decor.

Faux cracked-stone blocks and a pillar bring a sense of antiquity to this living room.

Textural Finishes

Nature is a world of different textures—the veins of a leaf, the crinkles of bark—and a home needs texture, too. Hard, flat walls tend to emphasize the impersonal look of some modern rooms, while adding texture brings interest and character into a home.

Opposite: Paint techniques are ideal for furniture as well as walls. This wardrobe and chest of drawers have been distressed by rubbing the paint down to the bare wood, creating depth and texture. Details of the two pieces have been accented in contrasting colors.

There are many ways to ensure that painted surfaces have texture to add an extra dimension to their look. Just as you have chosen colors to match the period and style of your home, you can also select a texture that matches the decor. You might go for the subtle, restrained classicism of stippling, or the rustic boldness of distressing the surfaces.

Whichever method you choose, practice the technique first, preferably on card that you can then put in the chosen location and study to see how it works in context. Some of these techniques do not forgive mistakes easily, so you need to be sure of what you are doing or employ a professional decorator.

Many traditional paint techiques have their origins in the great homes of the European aristocracy and were later spread by the merchant classes who wanted to share in their splendors. For example, the technique of dragging was developed in eighteenth-century France by those trying to simulate the look of genuinely silk-lined walls that they had seen in great houses. Other effects have an entirely different intention. Distressing or antiquing are designed to mimic the rustic or faded-splendor effect of aging materials.

Choose furniture and accessories to match your paint technique. For example, crackling was developed in eighteenth-century France. It evokes the look of age often seen on Renaissance frescoes or paintings. Modern furniture would be quite out of place, but an eclectic mix of antiques combined with richly patterned rugs and brocades will complete the look. In contrast, the sun-bleached effect of liming is ideal with rustic-style furniture and florals.

...ing simulates the effect of aging and can
... and welcoming, like an old friend. It can be
...ood, and other surfaces to suggest the fading,
...d dappling caused by time and sunlight.

Suitability

Antiquing creates a two-tone look that imitates the effects of time on the chosen surface, which can be wood (the most common), plaster, and even plastic. Antiquing can be practiced on new furniture that might otherwise look out of place in a period decorative scheme. The technique is also useful on damaged pieces such as those with cracks, splits, and other markings: the technique will bring back their charm as the faults become part of their character.

Materials

Depending on the technique chosen, primer, latex paint, special toner glaze, and steel wool or some other abrasive

Cost and time

Cost: Moderate; Time: Moderate

Left: Antiquing has been used on the wood, plaster, and metal surfaces to re-create the imperfections of time.

Do it yourself?

Sand the surface until bare, and apply a coat of primer. Or for a really worn effect, move straight to the next stage of applying a base coat of latex paint. When it is dry, roughly apply a second color, wiping it before it dries to create imperfections. Alternatively, apply a coat of wax and paint over that, or brush on a special toner glaze, which ages the surface. In all cases, seal the surface with varnish or non-yellowing polyurethane.

Above: For this natural effect, choose earth-tone colors, such as terra-cottas, browns, and beiges, and tarnished-metal colors such as gold and pewter.

Colorwashing

Colorwashing is one of the simplest painting techniques, offering an alternative to flat colors by producing a mottled, swirly finish that adds texture and depth to its surface. Its origins are in the subtle tones created by broken-color techniques of fine art.

Suitability

Colorwashing is used mainly on walls, though it can be applied to wood. It is suitable for both period and modern interiors, and is especially popular in kitchens, where you may want to avoid blocks of flat color, which show the signs of wear. Colorwashing is good as an aging or shading technique, and will flatter the texture of roughly plastered walls. One of its benefits is that, as you build up layers from light to darker tones, you can alter the finish later on by adding an extra layer.

Materials

Watered-down latex paint, or gloss paint thinned with mineral spirits, or diluted PVA and powder paints

Cost and time

Cost: Low; Time: Moderate

Left: Colorwashing the wall gives it textural interest and depth in this minimalist study.

Do it yourself?

Practice first on a piece of wallpaper. Apply a base coat of the lighter color. Thin down the paint for the next layer (better to over- rather than under-dilute), and apply it with broad, random brush strokes or with a cloth as if washing the wall. Add a little more paint to your mixture; then apply layers until you are happy with the effect, softening any brushstrokes with a damp brush or cloth.

Above: This technique can be used to soften the effect of bold colors, such as citrus yellow, leaf-green, sky blue, and baby pink. Over the initial pale color, apply richer, darker shades for a dappled effect.

Combing

This technique of dragging the teeth of a comb through wet paint can mimic both wood grain and the opulent sheen of silk. The striped patterns created stretch the apparent height or width of the surfaces painted.

Suitability

This technique requires a very steady hand, and mistakes are hard to correct, so combing is most easily applied in small areas. It is suitable for walls, doors, and border areas, and for bringing new life to old cabinets and wardrobes. It can be used to make vertical, horizontal, or angled stripes, or curves or patterns such as plaid and basketweave. Combing in small sections, such as beneath a chair rail, creates a formal effect. The best results tend to be when the base color is white or neutral. The top color will always dominate.

Materials

Special metal or rubber comb, paint diluted to slow drying time

Cost and time

Cost: Low; Time: Moderate

Left: These wide stripes in terra-cotta and cream create a formal but welcoming effect.

Do it yourself?

First apply the basecoat, and allow it to dry. Ideally, the combing is a two-person job, as one can brush or roll a little diluted paint onto the surface while the other follows behind, pulling the comb through the wet paint. Clean the comb with a damp paper towel after each scrape to prevent paint from lingering on the comb and spoiling the neat, clean lines. Practice on a dry wall or a piece of cardboard first.

Above: You can combine two bright colors, such as orange and royal blue, if using this technique on a small area. But for larger areas, the effect works best when the base color is pale and the upper color harmonizes with it.

Crackling

Crackling creates cracks on painted surfaces, giving them the crazed-varnish look of old fine art and Renaissance frescoes. The technique is best done in period colors, on antique furnishings or tired-out furniture in need of a fresh look.

Suitability

Crackling requires speedy and controlled work, so it's best done in small sections, usually on wood. It can also work on plaster, stone, and plastic. It is a tricky technique that can produce spectacular results, transforming tired or mundane surfaces into period pieces. There are two approaches. Crackling uses water-based materials and creates an abstract cracked pattern. Craquelure uses oil paints and results in a finer network of tiny cracks.

Materials

Brushes, crackle glaze (water or oil-based), varnish

Cost and time

Cost: High; Time: High

Left: Crackling has created a marvelously aged effect on the russet paint below the chair rail.

Do it yourself?

Apply a coat of water-based latex paint in the color that you want to show through the cracks. When it is dry, paint crackle glaze in one direction over it. When that dries, coat with latex paint in the second (top) color. For craquelure, start with water-based eggshell; then apply two layers of special glaze. In both cases you can speed up drying with a hair dryer, and you must protect the finish with varnish.

Above: Because this effect mimics the crazing of Renaissance frescoes, try colors that evoke that period. For example, royal blue with gold underneath will resemble the look of Italian palazzi.

Distressing

Distressing is a set of simple techniques for making surfaces look weather-worn and old. Distressed plaster, wood, and metal create a sense of the past and are particularly suitable for rustic, exotic or Mediterranean schemes.

Suitability

Wood, plaster, and metal can all be distressed. The look particularly suits country-style interiors, creating a sun-cracked and relaxed feel. It can be used on both new and old furniture. Be selective about what and how you distress for the most natural effect. For example, distress the fronts of chair legs and the edges of tables, which naturally take more punishment than other areas. Newly exposed floors that seem too well preserved for their surroundings can also benefit from a little artificial wear and tear.

Materials

Grit paper, hammer, chisel, wire brushes, and a coarse file

Cost and time

Cost: Low; Time: Low

Left: The distressed wood paneling in this cottage-style room blends well with the simple wooden furniture.

Do it yourself?

Consider which parts of the surface would eventually show wear or suffer blemishes. Apply a base coat that blends with your decor, leaving random patches bare if you wish. Sand down areas to simulate their being worn down. Weather edges by rubbing them with a coarse file. To create dents, use a chisel or hammer. Work slowly and try not to overdo the effect: you want it to look worn, not worn out.

Above: Distressing suits a rustic New England or Scandinavian style. Both make strong use of pastel colors. Distressing takes away the sweetness of pastel shades, leaving them weathered and relaxed.

Dragging

Dragging is a technique for creating a subtle texture of irregular lines. The effect was especially popular in 1930s English country houses, where only slightly contrasting colors were normally used for a very subdued result. The effect is quietly elegant and nostalgic.

Suitability

Dragging was originally intended to evoke the look of silk-lined walls, and it can still lend an air of majesty to walls, doors, and furniture. Depending on the brush technique and glaze used, it can take the place of slightly textured wallpaper in living and dining rooms, and add a little panache to kitchen cabinets. Although commonly identified with country houses, it also suits the delicacy of classical-style interiors, or can be used to add texture to contemporary styles.

Materials

Dragging brush (or try fine-grade wirewool), oil-based glaze or paint

Cost and time

Cost: Low; Time: Low

Left: The aqua top coat has been dragged over a neutral base to make these robust lines.

Do it yourself?

This is a simple technique to master, and the glazes are fairly slow-drying, so there is not too much time pressure. The surface must be smooth, with all dents removed—indentations will show in the pattern. Brush or roll the surface with thinned oil-based paint or glaze. Then drag the brush from top to bottom in slow, continuous strokes, cleaning the brush after each pass.

Above: For a 1930s feel, opt for muted shades such as browns, deep blues, terra-cottas, and burgundies. Team them with narrowly differentiated harmonizing colors.

Dry Brushing

Dry brushing has been used for centuries by artists who want colors to "float" in a painting like wispy clouds in a blue sky. Now the technique has been taken up by decorators to create a delicate texture that can provide a strong backdrop.

Suitability

Dry brushing is effective on walls, tabletops, and other furniture. It provides texture for modern interiors, but can also be used to create an aged finish in period settings. As it requires broad, sweeping strokes, the easiest areas to use this technique on are large sections of wall, but dry brushing also subtly highlights architectural moldings. A few random sweeps will leave just a suggestion of misty color, while brushing over again in different directions (crosshatching) adds to the depth of the texture created.

Materials

Paint and an old, worn brush (or a new one with long bristles)

Cost and time

Cost: Low; Time: Moderate

Left: This dry-brushed wall has a subtle mottled texture that blends well with other colors and styles.

Do it yourself?

This technique sounds easy but requires a very light touch, so practice it first. Paint a light base coat, and let it dry. Dip your brush in the top coat, and brush most of it out onto a board so that your brush is almost dry. Holding the brush firmly near the bristle, graze in different directions over the wall surface, flicking the bristles lightly across it, leaving only a few wisps of paint as you move on.

Above: Dry brushing is best done with two colors of strongly contrasting tone, such as a light blue and a rich China blue.

Frottage

Frottage is a technique using two layers of paint or glaze and some paper to create a mottled pattern in which broken-up colors merge into a soft, natural effect. It is named after the French word for "rubbing," although this method is also known as fratting.

Suitability
Frottage works best on large spaces, usually walls or tables, and in large rooms—the full effect is best seen from a distance. Because everyone will do it slightly differently, every effect will be unique, but its results look a bit like weathered leather, as two colors merge and separate in random blotches. The final look is fresh and dramatic, so it can work well as part of a neutral scheme. It can be used to create a shading pattern where parts of the surface are left darker than others, so you can create contrast on your walls.

Materials
Base coat of paint, glaze, and greaseproof paper

Cost and time
Cost: Low; Time: High

Left: Every frottage finish is different, yet all create a soft but dramatic backdrop to a room.

Above: Frottage can create a dramatic effect akin to that of weathered leather, so it works well with simple neutral color schemes, such as olives, browns, and flesh tones.

Do it yourself?

A light base coat is applied and allowed to dry. Then a wet, darker glaze is painted on in small sections and removed with the paper. Because drying times are short, it is best to use two people: one painting, the other spreading crumpled paper into the glaze and rubbing it off. Some decorators opt for brown craft paper or tissue paper. After drying, finish the technique with protective varnish.

Glazes

Glazes are the essential ingredient in a number of paint effects, such as ragging and marbling. A glaze is a translucent tinted film, which is painted over a base coat and removed to create a pattern. Glazes provide rich, glowing warm tones to many surfaces.

Suitability

Also known as scumble, glazes bring a sumptuous, antique glow. They are suitable for many styles of decor, period and modern, but the Victorians were particularly fond of glazed tiles and wallpapers. The technique gained popularity in the 1930s and 1940s as an inexpensive alternative to wallpaper. Glazes are suitable for furniture and walls, and for small and large areas, including moldings and baseboards. They can be used to create modern patterned effects or simply to age a surface.

Materials

Glazes can be bought ready-made or prepared on site

Cost and time

Cost: Moderate; Time: High

Left: Glazes allow you to rag roll, as on the walls, and to age surfaces like the picture frame.

Do it yourself?

Surfaces must be very smooth and even: glazes will highlight any blemishes and indentations. Apply two coats of base paint to ensure full coverage. Only use water-based glaze on water-based paints. Oil-glaze will work on any base coat. Apply the glaze with a brush in small sections; then remove it using your chosen method, wiping away mistakes before they dry.

Above: Glazes can create strong, opulent effects and suit rich colors. Turn to Victorian color schemes of purples and golds.

Liming

In the sixteenth century, people would rub lime powder onto their furniture to discourage fungus, worms, and beetles. The white paste nestles in the grooves of the wood grain, producing a sun-bleached, whitened effect that is popular today.

Suitability

Liming lightens the look of wood, and especially softens the hard lines of dark woods such as oak, ash, and elm. It is particularly effective on carved surfaces and open-grained wood (so it is rarely used on pine). Liming is used to age yet simultaneously enliven doors, floors, and furniture. The look is very popular in kitchens and bathrooms, where it provides a mellow sheen while accentuating the visual interest of the wood grain and softening the harsh lines of the fittings.

Materials

Wire brush, liming paste, polishing cloth

Cost and time

Cost: Low; Time: Low

Left: Liming is especially effective on paneling, lightening the look and disguising the hard lines.

Do it yourself?

Lime is very nasty stuff, so today liming paste or wax, which is pushed into the grooves of the grain, is substituted. You want these as deep as possible, so accentuate them by rubbing with a wire brush. Remove all dust; then brush or rub in liming wax or paste, masking any areas you do not want affected. Wipe away any overspill, and buff to finish. Add a little black spattering to age the effect if you wish.

Above: Limed wood is well teamed with the pastels of Scandinavian Neoclassical style, such as eggshell blue, pink, dusty green, and lilac.

Ragging

Ragging is a technique which uses fabric to apply or remove a top coat, creating a textured finish of broken-up color. The end result looks aged or modern, depending on the colors used, and gives the impression of crushed velvet.

Suitability

Ragging is mainly used on walls, especially old ones that have developed the odd bulge. It is especially effective when stone colors are used, as the technique replicates the patterns of stone. Ragging can also be used very effectively on furniture such as chests and doors. If you choose period colors, it takes the room back in time, but it also works as part of a contemporary design, adding texture to the backdrop. Ragging off produces a softer look than ragging on.

Materials

Two or three paint colors and lots of rags or other fabrics such as towelling, leather, or plastic bags

Cost and time

Cost: Low; Time: Moderate

Left: Ragging on allows you to create repeating patterns that look a little like printing.

Do it yourself?

Fill and smooth all cracks. Apply a base coat of latex or eggshell paint. If ragging on, prepare your fabric first by crushing it several times to create folds and character. Brush a small section of top coat, and press the twisted dry rag onto the surface, removing the wet glaze. If ragging off, twist the rag and dampen it in the top coat, pressing it firmly on in a repeating pattern, working down the wall.

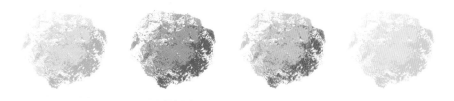

Above: Choose two similar colors for the best effects. Although ragging can create period effects, it can also create a very modern feel—these contemporary colors will bring the technique into the twenty-first century.

Sponging

Sponging creates a subtly dappled effect that suits contemporary settings but can provide an unobtrusive backdrop in period schemes where flat color provides insufficient texture or a blend of colors would complement the look.

Suitability

Sponging can be applied to any surface, especially plastered walls, doors, and furniture. Although it is a modern technique, it suits many styles of decor. Use brown and gray, and its mottled look can suggest stone. Pastel shades will create a feeling of airy brightness, while bolder, related colors create a deep, rich effect. Sponging in stages allows you to blend several colors in layers to add depth and to unify a multi-color scheme. This is a very inexpensive and easy technique that suits a beginner and produces reliable results.

Materials

Water- or oil-based paint, seawater sponge, paint tray, and card stock

Cost and time

Cost: Low; Time: Low

Left: The olive sponged wall is ideal for this neutral contemporary scheme of beige, brown, and green.

Do it yourself?

When the light base coat has dried, dampen the sponge and dip the frilly side in the darker top coat. Print it onto card stock to get rid of excess paint and test the print. Starting from the middle of the wall, start sponging on the paint, twisting your hand to keep the pattern random. You can also sponge off by removing the top glaze with a dry sponge, so experiment first to decide the best method for you.

Above: Sponging suits contemporary neutral schemes, such as the browns, creams, blues, and greens shown here. Using paler shades will have a subtler, more natural effect than using more contrasting, richer tones.

Staining

Staining is a way of altering the color of wood without concealing the beauty of the natural grain. This very simple technique will suit country-style decor and any decorative scheme where the accent is on natural finishes and textures.

Suitability

Any wood can be stained, and staining can suit any look or color scheme. Prime candidates for staining are large areas such as paneling or floors with an attractive grain that you don't want to cover up with paint. Wooden furniture is often stained. If the wood itself is attractive, a clear stain will suffice. However, if it has lots of knots, a colored stain will enhance it and can complement your color scheme. A more ambitious scheme is to create a pattern using different-colored stains.

Materials

Oil- or water-based wood stain, and a paint brush

Cost and time

Cost: Moderate; Time: Moderate

Left: This rustic-style sideboard has been stained different colors and then painted over.

Do it yourself?

The surface must be stripped down to the bare wood, and knots will need sealing so they do not leak resin. Always test the stain on a sample of the same wood as it can be tricky finding a good color match, and much depends on the darkness or lightness of the original wood. Apply the stain sparsely, as runs and spills will show in the finish and too much coating stops the stain drying.

Above: In American Colonial homes, wood was normally painted dark green, soldier blue, or burgundy. Try staining your wood the same shades for an authentic period look.

Stippling

Stippling is one of the most subtle, and tricky, of the paint techniques. Before deciding on a color combination, look at pointillist paintings by artists such as Seurat to see how colors in dot form work when placed next to one another.

Suitability

Stippling can be used on paneling, furniture, frames, carvings, and of course walls. Cinemas and cocktail bars of the 1930s were often decorated with stippling in three or four colors, which creates an atmospheric, smoky effect. However, the technique is just as appropriate for neoclassical schemes and modern decor, provided you are not looking for something that is dramatic in itself. The drama comes in the application: it takes a steady hand and much care to produce stippling's gently mottled backdrop.

Materials

Oil- or water-based glaze, and stippling brush or similar brush

Cost and time

Cost: Low; Time: High

Left: Duckegg-blue stippling has created a surprisingly delicate effect in this modern kitchen.

Do it yourself?

Your surface must be flawless because stippling will emphasize any imperfection. A stippling or stencil brush is best, but good results can be achieved with brooms on large areas and shoe brushes elsewhere. Whatever you choose, practice with it first. Oil glaze will give you more working time and a more subtle texture. Lightly tap the brush onto the surface to leave little flecks on it. Do the edges first.

Above: Choose your colors carefully with this technique because it can create odd optical effects. Test out your scheme first. Pretty pastels and subtle neutrals suit this delicate effect well.

Faux Techniques

The possibilities for faux techniques are endless: you can transform wood into stone, paper into metal, plastic into gold, and plaster into animal skin. No wands are required: just paint, brushes, rags, sponges, and above all, imagination.

Opposite: Faux wooden paneling has been created below the chair rail. The pale pine effect teams well with the white wall and neutral scheme. The feel is simple but rich in texture.

Faux finishing is the art of making a surface look as if it's made of another material. Faux techniques have been around for thousands of years. The ancient Egyptians used faux techniques on their tombs, the Incas on their jewelry, and the Romans on their walls. In the last few centuries there have been fads for fake stone, leather-look panels, wood-grained walls, and gilt-effect screens, all achieved with clever tricks to avoid carting costly and heavy materials across continents.

Today, faux techniques help you make your home truly individual. Whatever your decorative scheme, there will be some trick to add texture, such as a velvet wall; visual interest, such as an instant mosaic for the bathroom; or grandeur, such as stone blocking in the dining room.

The key to successful decoration with faux techniques is to practice first: on cardboard or a wood panel, or on a sample of whatever surface you'll be painting. You'll get a feel for how hard to press that sponge, how much paint those rags will take off in one swipe, and how much glaze a comb can drag. Another crucial element is to prepare the surfaces first. Few things can be more frustrating than standing back to admire your painstakingly marbled wall and noticing a hole that should have been filled and sanded yesterday. Alternatively, if you feel less confident of your skills or you don't have the time to decorate yourself, consider hiring a professional decorator to create these looks for you.

Many of the techniques in this chapter have their origins in days gone by, but they don't just have to be part of a period scheme. All these techniques can add richness to any contemporary look.

Animal-Skin Effect

If you're looking for something that makes a huge impact, go for painted zebra stripes or leopard skin. These effects are big, bold, and guaranteed to get people talking about your decorating scheme. Their outrageous impact may not be to everyone's taste, but you can't ignore them!

Suitability

Leopard and zebra skin work in small sections and small spaces. So if you choose this for the living room, do it along one wall or one section. Leopard-skin fans also like to employ the effect in small rooms such as cloakrooms and bathrooms, and its bold impact can suit children's rooms, too. The effect complements other leopard-skin or animal designs on fabrics and accessories. For colors, use brown, black, khaki, or gold with white or cream, or employ one of the bold hues of your modern theme, alongside a neutral.

Materials
Pencil, paint, household sponge

Cost and time
Cost: Low; Time: Moderate

Left: For a cloakroom or bathroom with impact, go for zebra skin, here in beige and brown.

Do it yourself?
Select colors that blend well with the rest of the room, as it is the pattern and contrast you want to accentuate most. For stripes, draw shapes onto the wall in pencil, perhaps copying a photograph or a fabric to get a mixture of patterns. If you want spots, apply them on top of a base coat using a household sponge. This also allows you to choose more than one top color, so experiment first.

Gilt

Usually delivering a gold finish, gilding has been a popular technique for giving the impression of wealth and luxury for centuries. Gilding is a means of transforming surfaces so that they appear to be coated with metal, shimmering with a rich glow as they catch the light.

Suitability

Gilding applies a thin layer or powder of gold, silver, platinum, bronze, copper, or other precious metals. It adds elegance and luster to wooden and plaster carvings, frames, vases, candlesticks, and any small object, even if it is made of humble plastic, turning a dull accessory into a shimmering symbol of luxury. Gilding is best used in small quantities to add a lift to a decorative scheme—too much gilding can look ostentatious. Gilded surfaces are also often aged to help them blend with period-style decor.

Materials

Gilding size, gilding leaf or powder, and gilding knife

Cost and time

Cost: High; Time: High

Left: This gilt finish has also been antiqued to fit with the period look.
Below: The gilding has been sponged.

Do it yourself?

Gilding requires time, patience, and skill. The easiest and cheapest technique is to use gilding powder. While it will not shine as brightly as gold leaf, it will still be superior to a painted finish. A base coat is required to seal and stabilize the surface, which must be totally free of dust and dirt. Powder can then be applied, and sealed when dry. Other options are gilding cream, and of course thin sheets of the metal required, probably gold. If using gold leaf, paint the surface with gold size and wait until it is almost dry before cutting the metal leaf and putting it in place with the long-bladed gilding knife. Gilded surfaces are often aged with antiquing glaze.

Granite Effect

A granite paint effect takes time but is an easy, technically undemanding way of adding texture and character to a surface. Granite has a wider, more subtle range of colors than other stones, so it can suit a variety of decorative schemes.

Suitability

A granite effect provides a sober, elegant backdrop that blends well with other finishes, such as the popular choice of a granite countertop in the kitchen. The technique is suitable for walls, pillars, fireplaces, and tabletops. The granite paint effect is achieved through sponging and speckling (or spattering) in granite-type colors such as gray, brown, rust, peach, green, silver, and black. With such a choice of colors, the granite effect blends with a range of color schemes and both period and modern styles.

Materials

Sea sponge and stippling brush or toothbrush

Cost and time

Cost: Low; Time: High

Left: A granite-effect wall teams with a genuine granite countertop.
Below: Granite effect in a dining room.

Do it yourself?

The surface should be clean and dry, but any dents and blemishes will look natural under the finish. Sponge a base layer of gray or light brown. Lightly sponge on other layers of suitable colors as listed above, allowing each layer to dry. The final coat will be spattered on, a technique that requires a little practice. Dip the stippling brush or toothbrush in the top-color paint; then remove any excess with a rag or newspaper. Holding the brush about 1 foot from the surface, gently flick the bristles to send tiny dots of paint onto the surface. You can choose whether to finish the effect with fake stone block lines, or leave it to look like a solid slab.

Lacquer

More than a thousand years ago, the Chinese were the only people able to use lacquer. Only they had access to the type of tree that produced a resin that, when painted onto a surface and sanded and repainted as many as a hundred times, created a mirror-like shine.

Suitability

Decorators of grand European houses in the eighteenth century admired the elegant finish of lacquer, but its high cost forced them to devise ways to simulate it on furniture. This technique was used on oriental-style cabinets, chests, and screens. The classic high-sheen lacquer finish is traditionally associated with the quintessentially Chinese colors of red and black, but today is used more widely where an elegant, polished finish is required, often as part of an Oriental-style scheme.

Materials

Oil- or water-based lacquer, also available in aerosol form

Cost and time

Cost: Moderate; Time: Low

Left: The lacquered finish of the gray-blue cabinet doors reflects light and brings to life this family kitchen.

Do it yourself?

Oil and water do not mix. So your lacquer must be made from the same base material as the coats which you are going to varnish. The surface must be completely smooth and free of dust. Apply like other varnishes. On small areas such as picture frames, two coats of black eggshell paint and a layer of varnish will make a good approximation of the lacquered effect— less trouble than a hundred coats!

Leather Effect

When used in decoration, leather looks grand, masculine, and sophisticated. It has the feel of a Victorian library or a neoclassical dining room. Real leather is very expensive, so the leather paint effect is a highly useful technique.

Left: Burgundy leather panels blend well with wooden shelving in this period-style library.

Suitability

Leather stretched over a flat surface such as a wall panel has been a mainstay of grand libraries and living rooms for centuries. The leather paint effect works well in similar settings: panels and wall sections in large rooms. It suits Gothic interiors, a sixteenth-century Tudor look, and modern settings as well. Try classic, sober period tones such as browns, greens, reds, and blacks, which can be teamed with complementary colors in most schemes.

Materials

Latex paint, oil scumble glaze, plastic bag or blank newspaper

Cost and time

Cost: Low; Time: High

Do it yourself?

The faux leather effect is achieved with the frottage technique. (See page 201.) Paint a base coat from your basic color scheme. Brown will create the most realistic rich leather effect, but red is also a striking choice. When it is dried, apply oil scumble glaze in a lighter color, perhaps cream; then wipe most of it off with the bag or blank newspaper, keeping the pattern regular.

Marble Effect

If you decide on a faux marble finish, you are in good company. The ancient Egyptians used it, as did the Romans, despite their ready access to the real material. This was because marble was difficult to transport and could not be used for beams and ceilings.

Suitability

Marbling is the most popular of the stone finishes. It was especially common in seventeenth-century France and Italy, and after a time, decorators experimented with a wider range of colors than the grays, pinks, and yellows of marble. The technique can be used on walls, paneling, architectural details such as fire surrounds, tabletops, and even floors. Its cool elegant tones are particularly popular for bathrooms. When choosing colors, use similar tones, as the subtle patterns of marble do not have much contrast.

Materials

Eggshell paint, oil-based glaze, softening brush, narrow brushes

Cost and time

Cost: High; Time: High

Above left: The marble-effect walls team perfectly with the true-marble column and white woodwork.

Do it yourself?

Different marbles vary in color, so select your main hue: white (Carrara), green (Serpentine), yellow (Siena), pink (Brescia), or gray (Fossilstone). Once, you needed distemper and gesso paints, but today a ready-made transparent oil glaze is painted over white or gray eggshell. On this slightly slippery surface you paint thin lines and dots for veins and patterns, then tease them out slightly with a soft brush.

Above: One wall has been treated in the distinctive golden yellow of Siena marble for a rich, warm backdrop.

Above: Classic marbling has a gray background with thin brown or black lines softened with a brush.

Metallic Looks

Metallic finishes can create a startlingly realistic effect of silver, copper, gold, and other metals in the most unlikely places. In natural light, metallics shimmer with their beautiful colors, and when evening comes they can dazzle with drama in the artificial light.

Suitability

You can apply a metallic finish to any surface that will take paint. The effect is an intriguing addition to the palette for modern decor, blending well with grays and neutrals, and holding its own against bold, bright colors. Metal finishes also suit the gothic style as panels or as stenciled motifs working as a border. The technique can work across whole walls, especially if you choose less-harsh finishes such as bronze or copper, but it is best employed as small blocks or in patterns.

Materials

Metallic finishes in latex or oil paint and as glazes; roller and brush

Cost and time

Cost: Moderate; Time: Low

Left: Blocks of subtly varied metallic paints have turned the wall into a piece of modern art.

Do it yourself?

Take time to choose the right metallic finish: latex paints will be easiest to use, but you can achieve more-realistic effects and oxidized finishes with oil-based paints, gels, glazes, and sprays. Whatever material you use, the biggest problem with metal finishes is hiding the brush strokes to achieve a smooth sheen. Practice first, and apply the paint with a short-pile roller if there is enough space.

Mosaic Effect

A painted mosaic creates an exciting decorative pattern that adds visual interest and texture. Tiled mosaics in which small pieces of stone or glass are arranged to make a picture or pattern have been popular since the Roman era. Save the expense and time by painting one instead.

Suitability

This technique can be used on any surface that takes paint, and in any place that would benefit from the addition of an intricate pattern or picture. Mosaics suit Mediterranean and classical styles, and are most popular in kitchens, bathrooms, and garden rooms, although they can also be effective in small sections of living rooms—for example, below chair rails or as borders. Of course, the Romans covered floors in tiled mosaics, and this effect will work for flooring, provided it is well sealed and protected.

Materials

Household sponge, latex paints, wooden block, and paint tray

Cost and time

Cost: Low; Time: High

Left: Mosaics make a pleasingly textured finish that can be patterned, pictorial, or plain, as here.

Do it yourself?

Cut an ordinary household sponge into shallow cubes with identical dimensions. Glue them to a wooden board to make a printing block. If the pattern is to have blocks of the same color, you can just dip this in a paint tray and apply. Otherwise you will need to paint the separate cube faces in the colors selected very fast and press it to the wall before the first ones dry. Seal with varnish.

Plaster Effect

Rough plaster walls are warm and rustic, evoking the sun-drenched walls of the Mediterranean. Bare plaster is dusty and easily stained, but painting a faux plaster effect allows you to create a lasting plaster finish in the color of your choice.

Suitability

This effect was very popular in French cafés of the 1970s, and it certainly suits large spaces where an air of rustic warmth is desired. This effect needs an airy room: it tends to make small rooms feel rather cramped. However, it is also suitable for making wooden or plastic moldings or ornaments match the plaster in the rest of a room, and for embellishing architectural details. Because you can use earthy tones for a natural look or bolder colors, this technique will work as part of just about any decorative scheme, modern or period.

Materials

Latex paints and a sponge

Cost and time

Cost: Low; Time: Moderate

Left: The effect of unpainted plaster has a natural, relaxed feel, and complements finishes such as wood.

Do it yourself?

Apply a base coat of latex paint in cream, terra-cotta, or other earthy hues (pink tints add warmth). When it dries, dampen in random patches and paint on a lighter shade of latex paint diluted half and half with water, leaving some sections bare. With a damp sponge, dab and sponge over this layer to create a mottled effect of gentle blurs. Protect heavily trafficked areas with matte varnish.

Rusting

If you want to add a darkly atmospheric element to your decor, rust effect may be the answer. Metal fittings and details tarnish and corrode over time, and faking this effect brings a sense of history to a setting, making it ideal for period styles.

Suitability

Rusting can be applied to any surface that will take paint. It suits medieval, Tudor, and baroque settings, but would also add a touch of mystery to a modern scheme. Rusting is a powerful effect best used in small amounts, perhaps on doors and certainly on baseboards, moldings, and ornaments. A kitchen with an urban look might suit rust-effect cabinet doors. The effect can be paired with genuinely rusty objects such as chains or fire tongs, which can be protected with beeswax.

Materials

Latex paints, fine sand, varnish, and methylated spirits

Cost and time

Cost: Low; Time: Moderate

Left: The rust effect on this modern wooden screen has created a richly textured effect and suits an urban style of decor.

Do it yourself?

Rust is an uneven finish, so you don't have to worry about your painting technique at all. If you want extra texture, first coat the surface with PVA (polyvinyl acetate water-based glue) and throw on some fine sand. Now brush on deep-brown latex paint, sponging on a layer of slightly lighter brown or red. Add random patterns with rust-colored latex if you wish. Coat with matt varnish.

Silk Effect

Silk is the film star of fabrics: it is guaranteed attention because of its sensuous good looks. The subtle sheen of silk has been used decoratively ever since the Chinese perfected making the material— and tried to keep the process secret from the rest of the world.

Suitability

Silk has been made for at least 5,000 years. Its texture and luster found favor with many civilizations: the Chinese themselves; the Egyptians used it on mummies; European and Asian cultures traded in it as a luxury for clothes and decoration. By the thirteenth century, Italian-made silk was rivaling the oriental supplies, and production began in the Americas in the seventeenth century. We can see from its history that silk was used as a decorative fabric in many eras, so it will work as part of any scheme. You can avoid the enormous expense of fixing silk onto panels and mounting them on the wall: just paint the wall instead. Silk is highly absorbant and can be dyed in particularly vivid colors. So while you could restrict yourself to the creamy neutrals of natural silk, any color, including bold exotics, will be suitable for a silk paint effect.

Materials

Special metal or rubber comb, paint, diluted to slow drying time

Cost and time

Cost: Low; Time: Moderate

Above left: A silk effect suits many rooms and styles. Here the natural creamy color chosen harmonizes with the marble basin surround.

Do it yourself?

Select your colors first. Since the effect suits any hue, choose one from the key colors in your scheme. If it is a bright color, consider only using the effect on one feature wall or panel section. If it is a neutral, the effect will not be too overpowering if used throughout the room. You may decide on a softer, mottled background, in which case use the sponging technique to build up your background layers. (See page 205.) If possible, get a partner to brush or roll a little diluted paint in your darker color onto the surface while you follow behind, pulling the comb through the wet glaze in long, continuous strokes. Clean the comb with a damp paper towel after each scrape to prevent paint from clinging to the comb and spoiling the neat, clean lines, which will give the impression of a silk finish. Practice on a dry wall or a piece of cardboard first, as mistakes are hard to correct.

Stone-Block Effect

Faux stone blocks are sober and elegant, bringing an air of strength and durability to a room. They can be used to give an imposing impression, to add a sense of theater, or as part of a trompe l'oeil scheme. (See page 190.)

Suitability

Faux stone blocks were fashionable in the eighteenth century because of their feeling of power and weight. The effect suits theatrical historical styles such as medieval and gothic, but can team with modern styles too, especially if paired with other stone effects such as marble. You can use a variety of stone colors, from granite grays to sandstone yellows or greenish marble. The most important element in the design is to get the size of the fake blocks in proportion to the room: too large or small, and the result will look awkward. It is also worth considering angling the blocks diagonally, as in two of these pictures, to lighten the effect.

Materials

Depending on the techniques being used: latex paints, sponge, rags, stippling brush, acrylic scumble glaze, and oil crayon

Cost and time

Cost: Moderate; Time: High

Above left: Faux blocks are cleverly blended with a plaster effect to suggest a renovated building.
Above right: Stone blocks fit in well as part of a grand baroque decorative scheme.

Do it yourself?

Many techniques can be used as part of the faux stone block effect. To begin, choose natural, earthy, or rock-like colors and decide which types of stone you will simulate, as they all have different characteristics. Paint on a latex wash in terra-cotta or a similarly deep neutral color. Add a lighter layer using random brush strokes or sponging or ragging techniques. Mark out the shape and size of the fake blocks with a pencil or chalk line. (Paint won't adhere to pencil so it will need rubbing out later.) Vary the sizes of the blocks to avoid too much regularity. Paint, rag, or sponge each block, darkening the edges. You could stipple them at this point to add texture: in which case mark each one out with decorator's tape. Add veins for a marble effect. (See page 215.) You can also shade the edges of each block with an oil crayon. Finally, paint in the mortar lines in gray or sand color, sealing the finish with matte varnish.

Suede Effect

The faux suede technique brings depth and richness to a room. The concept of fabric wallhangings dates back millennia, and a suede effect provides that feel of luxury and comfort while adding to the textures of the room.

Suitability

This is a striking effect best suited for use on feature walls where a warm, welcoming texture is required. It would suit rustic or modern interior styles, and could even fit in a period setting in place of the more formal leather look. The finish is not hardwearing so it will not suit high-traffic areas. Suede paint catches and reflects the light differently according to the random brush strokes with which it was applied, so it will be a major point of interest in a room. It will also complement suede or textured furnishings and fabrics.

Materials

Pre-prepared suede paint, wide brush, possibly also a wool roller

Cost and time

Cost: High; Time: Low

Left: The suede-effect panels have a formal effect in this dramatic living area.

Do it yourself?

The wall must be smooth and dust-free. The pre-prepared suede paint is applied in two coats with a large brush, roller, or sponge. The second coat should be applied in irregular crisscrossing strokes. This will determine how light is reflected from the surface to give the two-tone, light and dark, raised impression of suede. Sealing the finish will change it to a velvet or gloss look.

Velvet Effect

For a sumptuous fake fabric look with echoes across much of history, go for velvet. It is particularly identified with the medieval and Renaissance periods, when the expense of its manufacture made it the preserve of royalty and the very rich.

Suitability

Velvet dates from 2000 B.C., when the Egyptians were making a material using a similar technique to that used today. They admired its thick, heavy pile, which later decorators found so useful for draping along walls to prevent drafts. In addition to its links with the medieval and gothic style, the velvet look features in decor from the Georgian, Victorian, and Art Deco periods. It is a sound choice for a textured living room, bedroom, or dining room wall effect to go with many color schemes.

Materials

Latex eggshell paint, rags or materials such as cotton, cheesecloth, and chamois leather

Cost and time

Cost: Low; Time: Moderate

Left: The moss-green velvet effect in this elegant sitting room creates interest and texture.

Do it yourself?

Classic velvet colors are royal blue, deep red, burgundy, emerald green, and gold. Make sure the wall surface is smooth, clean, and dust-free. Apply two base coats of latex eggshell in your choice of color. When dry, paint on a slightly lighter shade of the color, or a neutral such as cream. Immediately wipe it off with a tightly rolled rag or other piece of fabric, leaving behind a mottled sheen effect.

Wallpaper Effect

If you are toying with the idea of painting your own design onto wallpaper, you are traveling back in time to the fifteenth century, when the first painstakingly hand-painted wallcoverings were introduced, using the then exciting new material, paper.

Suitability

Painting your own paper can form part of a decorative scheme from many eras. Wallpaper was a rich person's material in the seventeenth and eighteenth centuries. In the 1600s, the nobility would have their coat-of-arms put into the design. One hundred years later, people began to glue paper over wooden boards and paint it to simulate expensive tapestry or paneling. The Victorians loved wallpaper, then being mass produced, and artists such as William Morris produced their own richly patterned designs.

Materials

Roller, primer, latex paint, and stencils or printing blocks

Cost and time

Cost: Low; Time: High

Left: This 1970s-style faux wallpaper effect in yellow and white has created a unique and playful look.

Do it yourself?

Apply a coat of oil-based primer or thinned undercoat. Test to see if colors are likely to bleed into the paper, and if they do coat with aluminum-based primer or thinned knotting. If you are hand-painting, mark out your design in chalk first (paint doesn't adhere on pencil). Alternatively, go for a repeating pattern using a stenciling or block-printing method, sealing it with varnish to finish.

Wood Graining

Wood graining is an inexpensive way to give the impression of wood, or to alter woods so they match others in a room. The technique was developed in the seventeenth century and reached the height of popularity in the nineteenth century, when dark wooden interiors were fashionable.

Do it yourself?

Wood graining is a relatively simple technique, but it is worth practicing on a board first to keep it realistic, basing your work on careful study of the graining pattern of the real thing, often expensive woods such as oak or mahogany. The surface should be filled and smoothed. Apply two coats of eggshell in a color such as terra-cotta and allow it to dry. Then apply the glaze in a darker brown. Water-based glazes dry very fast so work in small sections. To create the graining effect, either use a dragging technique or a narrow brush. (For dragging, see page 199.) Add wriggles to simulate the pattern of real grain, and you can even create knots with a blob of glaze, which you then drag a little. Subdue the overall effect with a long-bristled softening brush. A pale wood finish that replicates whiter woods such as maple or satinwood uses a similar technique, with a water-based glaze, and is known as *clair bois*.

Suitability

Wood graining works on any surface that will take the eggshell paint used as a base coat. So it can be used to make materials like plastic or hardwood resemble wood, and to make one wood look like another. In a room with a handsome dark mahogany chest, you might choose to wood-grain the lighter, cheaper wooden doors or paneling to match the more expensive and attractive material. The technique can also be used to create a fake baseboard or a chair rail on a plaster wall, for example. Very old and worn floorboards that really need painting to conceal their faults can also be treated in this way. With practice, you can simulate different kinds of wood very effectively, adding knots and even typical blemishes to make the wood in a room seem as if it all came from the same type of tree at the same time. Most people choose natural wood colors, but you can use others if you wish.

Materials

Oil- or water-based glaze, dragging brush, and a softening brush

Cost and time

Cost: Low; Time: Moderate

Above left: Wood graining allows you to create realistic wood effects to match other surfaces such as floors.

Practical Checklist

CHOOSING PAINT

Paint is the easiest and least expensive medium to use in decorating. It is also one of the most satisfying, because you can transform a room in a day. However, painting does require careful planning and allocation of time. Decorators say that 90 percent of the work is in the preparation, not wielding a paint brush.

Choosing a decorating scheme

There is plenty of advice in this book on choosing colors and paint techniques, beginning on page 14. However, it's worth going over a few pointers:

- Get samples of the paints you are considering using. Paint them onto cardboard or in patches on the walls.
- Look at your sample boards in different light conditions.
- Remember that paint always changes color as it dries: usually it gets darker.
- Follow your instincts and use colors you like, not what you think you should like. Don't feel you have to go bold or bright just to be contemporary.

- Feel confident about—and carry through—the effect you would like to create, whether that's modern, traditional, feminine, or bold.
- Unless you are completely overhauling your decorative scheme, consider what colors are already being used in the room in furnishings and accessories, and try to weave them into your scheme.
- Consider the amount and quality of natural light in your room. Would the room benefit from sunnier colors, for example?
- Are you happy with the size of your room—would you like it to seem larger or more cozy? Would you like to enhance or disguise any features in your room? For ideas, see "Enhancing Your Space," which starts on page 154.
- Take into account not only color contrasts and accents but tone and texture. Most schemes benefit from a variety of tonal values and textures.
- Have you considered a period or exotic scheme? If you opt for a dramatic look, consider how you will carry that scheme through in the furnishings and accessories in the room.

TYPE OF PAINT	LOOKS/CHARACTERISTICS	SURFACES	TYPES OF ROOM
Flat or low-gloss latex	Dull, matte finish; not hardwearing or easy to clean	Walls and ceilings	Master bedrooms, formal dining rooms
Semigloss latex	Shiny; hardwearing and wipeable	Walls, ceilings, and trim	Children's rooms, kitchens, bathrooms, laundry rooms, pantries
Eggshell/ Satin finish	Between matte and gloss; durable	Walls and woodwork	Children's rooms, entryways, stairways, bathrooms, family rooms
Alkyd (oil) paints	Shiny; hardwearing and washable	Wood and metal	Doors, chair and picture rails, wooden and metal accessories
Varnish	Can be shiny or matte; hardwearing	Bare wood and some painted surfaces	High-traffic areas such as entryways
Wood stain	Natural or colored	Wood	Bare wooden surfaces such as furniture and low-traffic areas

- If you feel that your room needs a little more than flat blocks of color, consider paint techniques. For real drama, choose a pattern, picture, or trompe l'oeil effect. If choosing one of these bold effects, consider whether the size and furnishings of your room will work well with it or be overpowered. Textural and faux effects can add depth and texture to your scheme. Consider how they will team with other textures and patterns in the room.

Types of paint

Once you've chosen your color scheme, it's time to decide on the type of paint to use. Factors to bear in mind include the following:

- What surface are you intending to paint? Choose recommended paints for wood and metal. You may need to use a primer or sealant when painting on surfaces such as wood, metal, and unpainted plaster. Primers are also used on surfaces that have been painted before but were repaired or are showing signs of wear such as flaking and peeling.
- Are you painting areas that need to be damp-proof or to resist heavy wear and tear, such as kitchens and bathrooms? Choose recommended kitchen and bathroom paints that are easily wipeable.
- Consider the level of sheen you want. This is the level of gloss or shininess. High-sheen paints reflect more light and have a harder finish that is often wipeable.
- If you're using a paint technique, your choice will often be limited to the paint types suitable for the task. (See specific entries for details, starting on page 176.)

Your final choice is between latex and oil paints. There are two basic types of paint: water-based (latex) and oil-based (alkyd-resin). A few years ago, the water-based paints were for walls and ceilings, and for wood or metal surfaces you used oil paints. However, paint technology is changing rapidly and there has been a big expansion in the range of surfaces on which different water-based paints can be used. As a general rule, oil-based paints are harder wearing but trickier to work with. (See the table on the opposite page.) Latex is low odor, easy to clean from equipment and mistakes, and quick-drying, and it can be recoated after about four hours. But it is hard to keep clean, stains easily, and is not durable in high-traffic areas. Oil-based paint has a glossy, hard-

TYPE OF PAINT OR FINISH	APPROXIMATE AREA COVERED BY ONE GALLON
Latex	87 square yards
Eggshell	87 square yards
Oil-based gloss	92 square yards
Varnish	85 square yards
Wood stain	120 square yards

wearing finish. It resists marking and is washable. Equipment and spatters must be cleaned with paint thinner. However, it usually needs an undercoat and more than one top coat. It is slow to dry and gives off a strong odor from solvents when drying.

How much paint?

To decide how much paint to buy, you first need to calculate the surface area to be covered. If you're painting walls, do this by multiplying the height of the room by its overall length (that's the length of all the walls added together). Work out ceiling areas by measuring the floor area.

One coat of latex paint will usually be enough for good coverage, depending on the manufacturer's recommendations. Oil-based gloss requires an undercoat, then at least one top coat. See the table, above, for approximating your paint needs. Buy each color in one go so that the batches are the same and you can avoid variations in shades.

What about wallpaper?

A popular idea is to combine areas of paint with areas of wallpaper: for example, below a chair rail or on a feature wall. This is ideal for creating interest or even experimenting with a boldly patterned paper without overpowering. Alternatively, you may decide not to use paint on your walls at all, if you don't like the mess of working with paint or prefer a uniformly patterned finish. Wallpaper can change the look of a room quickly and dramatically, and there is a huge range of coverings from which to choose. In addition, if your walls are in poor condition, you could apply wallpaper liner and paint over it. Or for a textured finish, you could paint over textured wallpaper.

When choosing patterned wallpaper, bear in mind the same color-scheme and pattern principles that you would consider when choosing paint colors and techniques. For example, large patterns tend to make a room seem smaller. Vertical stripes give an impression of height. Different patterns on either side of a chair rail can create interest. Borders can complete a look and offer a formal finish.

There are numerous types of wallcoverings:

- Wallpaper liner prepares rough walls for paint and wallcovering.
- Standard wallpaper is usually machine printed. It's a popular choice. The heavier the paper, the higher its quality.
- Washable wallcoverings, such as vinyl or vinyl-coated paper, can be wiped clean, so they are ideal for children's rooms.
- Embossed paper and blown vinyl have a decorative relief finish.
- Paintable textured coverings are made from linseed oil and flax, which is fused onto paper to create a hardwearing, paintable surface.
- Flock wallcoverings have a relief pattern creating a raised, velvet-like finish.
- Some natural textile coverings, such as burlap, are hardwearing and highly textured.

DOING IT YOURSELF

If you undertake your decorating work yourself, you will of course save a lot of money. You will also get a strong sense of achievement from transforming your home with your own hands, and will have the confidence to do it again in other rooms at other times. However, before picking up that brush, consider these questions:

- Have you got the skills to achieve the quality of work you want?
- Have you got the equipment?
- Have you got time? It will take much longer than you may imagine to buy the equipment, prepare your room, and then complete the painting itself.
- Can anyone help you? Many jobs, such as wallpapering, are much more easily done by two people.
- Could you do the basic work and then hire a professional decorator for the tricky parts, such as a complex paint technique?
- Where will you store your materials and equipment?

And finally, doing it yourself probably means working room by room rather than giving the whole floor or house a makeover. So you might have to scale down your project to make it achievable in the time you have.

Setting a budget

Write a list of everything you will need, including paint, wallcovering, tools, and preparatory materials. A tour of a home center or paint store or some internet research will give you a fair idea of what it will all cost. The biggest investment will be your time.

Use the table on the previous page to calculate the quantities of paint you will need. If you are buying equipment, it will obviously be usable for more than one job provided you look after it, so the outlay may be comparatively low.

Special paints, such as metallic finishes or pre-prepared glazes, are expensive compared with the cost of latex paints, but you will be buying relatively small quantities of these. Some techniques, such as gilding, require expensive materials, but most do not.

Wallcovering varies enormously in price, depending on the quality of the paper. Washable wallcovering costs more than the ordinary kind. Inexpensive wallcovering may be prone to fading.

Before you start

Good decorators spend longer on preparation than painting, because imperfect surfaces result in poor paint finishes. Bear in mind the following tips on preparation:

- Protect furniture and floors before you start preparing surfaces. Dust gets everywhere!
- Remove or seal up electrical equipment, such as the TV and sound system. Dust will damage them.
- If you can, roll up the carpets to at least 2 feet from the wall.
- Tape plastic bags over fixtures such as wall sconces, removing bulbs first.
- Fill small holes and cracks with joint compound; then lightly sand them smooth. This is a dusty, time-consuming job, but it's the only way to get a smooth surface.
- Scrape off flaking paint and sand the surface.
- Seal knots in bare wood to prevent resin from seeping through in a few months.
- Always wipe down sanded surfaces before painting. If you are using alkyd paints, do this with a cloth dampened with mineral spirits.

Painting tips

- Choosing the right equipment for the job is key. (See the table below.)
- The most sensible order of painting is to start with ceilings, then deal with walls, and finish with the woodwork and metal surfaces.
- Try to paint in natural light so that you can spot uneven patches and messy strokes.
- Don't overload the brush with paint, and keep the brush gliding across the surface, working away from the wet areas to keep the finish solid.
- Paint edges first; then work away from them across the surface.
- Always paint with the windows open to aid drying and to allow chemicals and odors to escape.
- Wear safety glasses when working on ceilings and using spray guns: swimming goggles are ideal because they have a tight seal.
- When you think you've finished, go out of the room and then come back in again to get a fresh perspective. You are bound to notice small blemishes to correct.

TOOL	USED FOR	COMMENT
Sandpaper	Smoothing surfaces	Comes in various grades: use fine grade for smoothing patched walls; for large areas, wrap the grit paper around a sanding block.
Joint knife	Filling small holes	Wipe clean after use.
Selection of different-sized paint brushes: ½ inch, 1 inch, 2 inch and 4 inch	Applying paint to small areas	Use small brushes for edges; wide brushes are for covering large areas of wall. Clean after use, or the bristles will get stuck together.
Paint bucket	Holding paint when you are on a ladder	
Paint roller and tray	Applying latex paint to walls and ceilings	Can be messy. The best rollers are lambswool; others are synthetic.
Paint pad and applicator	Painting large areas	
Paint sprayer	Painting large areas	Can be rented
Ladder		Must be stable
Drop cloths	Protecting furniture and carpets from spatters	
Mineral spirits	Thinning and cleaning alkyd paints	
Decorator's or masking tape	Protecting areas or surfaces from paint	Useful around windows and trim
Goggles	Protecting eyes	
Mask	Protecting lungs	

It is important to take good care of your equipment to get the most from it:

- Lay plastic wrap over paint before sealing it up: it stops paint from drying out and thickening.
- Don't hammer down paint-tin lids: rest a piece of wood across the top, and tap it down to ensure a proper seal.
- Label paint tins with their color and the location where the paint was used. This will save hours of puzzling over them later on if you need to touch up damaged areas.
- If you are taking a break, put wet brushes in a plastic bag. This stops them from drying out.
- Wash latex paint equipment in warm water with a little detergent; then rinse with water.
- Wash alkyd-paint equipment in mineral spirits.
- Keep brushes in good shape by wrapping them in newspaper to dry. It stops the bristles from spreading.

Wallpapering tips
Most wallpapering jobs are easier with two people to do the work. The key is to organize all the equipment and keep the working area tidy. Here are a few wallpapering tips:

- Few walls are truly straight, so use a plumb line to mark out the true vertical.
- Measure the wall height and cut your paper four inches longer to allow for fitting.
- When using patterned paper, check for pattern match before cutting the next roll.
- Brush paste from the center to the edges.
- Lightweight papers and vinyls can be hung after pasting. Heavy papers need to absorb the paste for about 10 minutes. Some vinyls are prepasted.

HIRING A PROFESSIONAL
If you decide that it will not be your hands clutching that paint brush, you need to hire someone to do it. Reasons to take this option might include:

- You know that doing the job right can't be achieved in the time you have available.
- You don't want to spend hours in home stores finding the right equipment and materials—you've got more exciting things to do with your time!
- You don't have the right painting and decorating skills and don't feel confident about taking on a major project. Maybe you don't know where to go for materials and equipment (or maybe nobody local can supply them) or how to use them for creating special paint effects.
- You don't know what you want. You need someone to help you develop your style.
- You have lots of ideas but are not sure if they would work and need someone to advise you and perhaps prepare room layouts so that you can see what they would look like. Or you may have a few ideas about individual rooms, but you haven't got the overall plan that will ensure a coherent scheme throughout your home.
- Your home dates from a particular period and you need advice about period colors and details.

You have a choice: paint and wallpaper contractor or interior designer. If you have a really clear idea of what you want, roughly what the materials will cost, and where most of the supplies will come from, go for a contractor. You don't need imaginative input from a contractor—you just want your scheme carried out to a professional standard. If you would like creative input, it's probably an

	CAN DO	CAN'T DO	ADVANTAGES	DISADVANTAGES
Paint and wallpaper contractor	All the practical interior decoration	Decide or advise on your scheme	Less expensive than a designer; offer all the do-it-yourself skills that you may be lacking	Limited design input; will need overseeing by you
Interior designer	Give you new ideas; supply labor; check technical details such as electrical safety		Will create a design scheme; will manage contractors	More expensive; the result may bear his or her hallmark more than yours unless you can communicate your ideas during the planning.

interior designer that you need. The table on the opposite page will help you decide who it is you should employ.

Finding and briefing a paint and wallpaper contractor

A contractor could be a single person or a small team. They are going to be in your house for a while, and their work is going to be in your home for considerably longer, so you need to feel completely confident in them and their abilities. Anyone can call themselves professional, so it's important to bear in mind the following pointers when deciding on the right one for the job:

- Ask for recommendations from friends or other local service providers.
- Consult a trade association for reliable professionals. The Painting and Decorating Contractors of America (PDCA) is a trade organization, but membership is voluntary.
- Look in local newspapers and community websites for advertisements and recommendations.
- When meeting with a potential contractor, ask for references from previous customers and follow them up. A true professional won't mind this at all.
- Ask to see photographic examples of work.
- If there are special paint effects in your design, hire a decorative painter. Again, ask to see examples of this work.
- Meet up a couple of times before offering the job. Feel confident that you can work with this person. He or she don't have to be your best friend, but you do need to feel you can be straightforward and honest.
- Ask for an estimate of what the job will cost and how long it will take.
- There's no substitute for a clear and agreed written brief, setting out the tasks to be completed.

Finding and briefing an interior designer

Take note of the advice above for finding a paint and wallpaper contractor, but in addition:

- If you've seen an interior you really like, ask who designed it and get in touch with that person.
- Only approach designers who work on residential projects—many of them specialize in offices, shops, public buildings, or other areas.
- In the US and Canada, most interior designers will have a qualification recognized by the National Council for Interior Design (NCID).

- You may want to check whether your designer is a member of a trade organization, such as the American Society of Interior Designers (ASID), the Interior Designers of Canada, or the Foundation for Interior Design Educational Research (IDEC).
- When talking to a potential designer, be clear what it is you need both from them and from the scheme itself.
- Be up front about your budget, and stick to it. If it becomes apparent that your budget will not stretch to what you want to achieve, you may need to rethink your plan or spread out the work over a number of years.
- Supply swatches, magazine clippings, and photographs to show fabrics, patterns, effects, and colors you like.
- Decide what furniture you definitely want to keep, and list it.
- Consider how you feel about room layouts and whether you want to keep them as they are or alter them.
- Be prepared for a dialogue. Part of a designer's expertise is in adapting your ideas into a practical scheme; that is what you are paying him or her for.

Costs and project management

Whomever you choose, be clear when conveying your ideas, and check the work as it goes along. If you are paying an hourly or daily rate rather than a flat fee, it is especially important that you do this efficiently, because indecision and lack of clarity soak up time, which will cost money.

- Agree whether you are to pay a flat fee, a day rate, or by the hour. Get this in writing.
- Agree what you will pay for, such as materials. Will you cover expenses?
- Your budget must include a contingency for unexpected costs.
- Agree when you will make payments. It is reasonable for professionals to have some money up front to pay for materials and disbursements, and for some of the fee to be held back until all the work is complete and satisfactory.
- Agree to a detailed plan, and then set up regular meetings to make sure everyone is sticking to it. These might be once or twice a week, depending on the length of the project.

Glossary

Accent color Contrasting color used in small proportions to draw the eye and add interest.

Antiquing Any technique that makes a surface look textured and aged.

Artist's brushes Fine-tipped brushes for intricate work.

Base coat The first coat of paint, which seals the surface.

Chair rail Trim running along a wall at chair height to prevent the moving of furniture from damaging the wall. Also known as a dado rail.

Color washing Painting technique in which layers of paint are added to suggest depth.

Combing Decorative technique in which a comb is dragged through wet paint or glaze.

Complementary colors Any pair of colors from opposite sides of the color wheel; e.g., green and orange. Also known as contrasting colors.

Cool colors The violets, blues, and greens from one side of the color wheel.

Crackle glaze Water-based glaze used under paint to create a peeling effect.

Decoupage French term for the technique of pasting and varnishing paper or fabric.

Distressing Imitating wear and tear by rubbing down.

Eggshell finish A semi-matte finish with low luster or soft sheen.

Enamel paint Smooth, quick-drying paint with a hard, glossy surface.

Fresco Picture created historically by painting onto wet plaster. Today the term is used to describe any picture painted onto a wall.

Frieze Lateral band decorated differently to the rest of a room, usually high on a wall.

Gilding Decorative technique giving a metallic appearance.

Glaze Transparent, tinted paint.

Grit paper Also called sandpaper—abrasive paper used to smooth surfaces.

Harmonizing colors Neighboring colors on the color wheel.

High-gloss finish Paint with a shiny finish, usually oil-based.

Lacquer Protective clear finish, applied in several thin coats.

Latex paint Water-based paint that is low in odor and easy to work with but is less durable than oil paints.

Liming Decorative technique of applying liming wax to create a soft, aged-looking finish.

Matte finish Also called flat—a dull, unshiny finish.

Oil-based paint Hard-wearing paint made from alkyd resin.

Palette Set of colors in a scheme.

Picture rail Molding high on a wall from which frames can be hung.

Primer A coating used to prepare surfaces, making them uniform.

Ragging Decorative technique using cloth to add or remove paint or glaze.

Satin finish Paint finish that is mildly shiny with little glare. Also known as semigloss.

Solvent Liquid, such as mineral spirits, used to thin and clean oil-based paints.

Spattering Decorative technique to spray dots of paint onto a surface.

Sponging Technique using a sponge to apply or remove wet paint.

Staining Technique of using oil- or water-based paints to add transparent color to wooden surfaces.

Stenciling Decorative technique of applying paint through cut card or film.

Stippling Paint technique in which specks of paint are applied.

Tint A color with white added to it.

Tonal value The lightness or darkness of a color.

Trompe l'oeil A painted effect that "tricks the eye," giving an impression of three-dimensional space.

Undercoat Protective layer of paint between primer and top coat.

Varnish Transparent protective finish.

Warm colors The reds, yellows, pinks, and oranges from one side of the color wheel.

Resource Guide

The following list of professionals, manufacturers, associations, and outlets is meant to be a general guide to industry and product-related sources. It is not intended as a complete listing of products and manufacturers represented by the photographs in this book.

ASSOCIATIONS

American Society of Interior
Designers (ASID)
608 Massachusetts Ave. NE
Washington, DC 20002-6006
Tel: 202 546 3480
www.asid.org

The Color Association
of the United States
Studio 507
315 West 39th St.
New York, NY 10018
Tel: 212 947 7774
www.colorassociation.com

Foundation for Interior Design
Educational Research
(FIDER)
Suite 1318
146 Monroe Center NW
Grand Rapids, MI 49503-2822
Tel: 616 458 0400
www.fider.org

Interior Design Educators Council
Suite 300
7150 Winton Dr.
Indianapolis, IN 46268
Tel: 317 328 4437
www.idec.org

Interior Designers of Canada
Suite 414
260 King St. E.
Toronto, ON M5A 1K3
Tel: 416 594 9310
www.interiordesigncanada.org

National Council for Interior Design
Suite 1001
1200 18th St. NW
Washington, DC 20036-2506
www.ncidq.com

The Painting and Decorating
Contractors of America (PDCA)
Suite 201
11960 Westline Industrial Dr.
St. Louis, MO 63146-3209
Tel: 800 332 PDCA
www.pdca.org

Paint and Decorating
Retailers Association
403 Axminister Dr.
Fenton, MO 63026-2941
Tel: 636 326 2636
www.pdra.org

Rohm & Haas Paint Quality Institute
P.O. Box 1348
Philadelphia, PA 19109
Email: info@paintquality.com
www.paintquality.com

INTERIOR DESIGNERS

Ambiance Interior Design
P.O. Box 175
Rye Beach, NH 03871
Tel: 888 999 5191
www.ambianceinteriordesign.com

Anna Rodé Designs, Inc.
17005 Castello Circle
San Diego, CA 92127
Tel: 858 759 2662
www.annarodedesigns.com

Annie Speck Interior Designs
Laguna Beach, CA 92651
Tel: 949 464 1957
www.anniespeck.com

Atelier Avant-Garde
2625 Chemin Ste.-Foy
Ste.-Foy, QC G1V 1T8
Tel: 418 651 1616
www.aag.qc.ca

Barbara Jacobs
Color and Design
53 Frairy St.
Medfield, MA 02052
Tel: 508 359 5753
www.integralcolor.com

Barry Senter Design
5135 Ballard Ave. NW
Seattle, WA 98107
Tel: 206 784 2597
www.barrysenterdesign.com

Bauer Interior Design
1286 Sanchez St.
San Francisco, CA 94114
Tel: 415 282 2788
www.bauerdesign.com

Björck Design
Tel: 425 922 3647
E mail: sandin@bjorckdesign.com
www.bjorckdesign.com

Bonnie MacArthur
Interiors, Inc.
57 St. Lawrence Place
London, ON N6J 2G4
Tel: 519 649 6531
www.bonniemacarthur
interiors.com

Bowerbird House Interiors
49 E. 73rd St.
New York, NY 10021
Tel: 212 988 6414
www.bowerbirdhouse.com

Casafina
Suite G
2307 Santa Clara Dr.
Santa Clara, UT 84765
Tel: 435 656 1677
www.casafinadesign.com

Chambers Interiors
and Associates, Inc.
2030 Irving Blvd.
Dallas, TX 75207
Tel: 214 651 7665
www.chambersinteriors.com

Cushing Terrell Architecture
and Interiors
221 Ninth Ave. N.
Seattle, WA 98109
Tel: 206 282 6222
www.cushingterrell.com

DBC Interiors
4239 Landmark Dr.
Orlando, FL 32817
Tel: 407 657 5484
www.dbcinteriors.com

Ellis and Paul Interiors
429 W. 46th St.
New York, NY 10038
Tel: 212 397 5400
www.epinteriors.com

Hillcrest Interiors
2907 Kavanaugh Blvd.
Little Rock, AR 72205
Tel: 501 664 3445
www.hillcrestinteriors.com

Inside Out Design
Suite 970
3044 Bloor St. W.
Toronto, ON M8X 2Y8
Tel: 416 253 5330
www.insideoutdesign.ca

Interiors Defined, Inc.
1221 North Orange Ave.
Orlando, FL 32804
Tel: 407 897 3220
www.interiorsdefined.com

International Interior Design
14 Sanderling Ave.
Irvine, CA 92604
Tel: 949 551 8726
Email: trudy@iidesign.net
www.iidesign.net

Jackson Interiors
1049 Montague Rd.
Park Hills, KY 41011
Tel: 859 261 9840
www.sjacksoninteriors.com

Judy Fox Interiors
Suite 101
4147 N. Goldwater Blvd.
Scottsdale, AZ 85251
Email: info@judyfoxinteriors.com
www.judyfoxinteriors.com

Julie O'Brien Design Group
Suite 195
11711 North College Ave.
Carmel, IN 46032
Tel: 317 706 0772
www.julieobriendesign.com

Karen Cole Designs
11416 North Bancroft Dr.
Phoenix, AZ 85028
Tel: 602 493 9154
www.karencoledesigns.com

Meyer Associates, Inc.
227 East Lancaster Ave.
Ardmore, PA 19003
Tel: 610 649 8500
www.meyer-associates.com

Paysage
3451 Fairmount Blvd.
Cleveland Heights, OH 44118
Tel: 216 397 8700
www.paysage.com

Reinboth and Company
121 North Union St.
Lambertville, NJ 08530
Tel: 609 397 2216
Email: reinboth@comcast.net
www.reinbothandcompany.com

Sally Curtis Starr
3980 Broadway #140
Boulder, CO 80304
Tel: 303 442 7704
Email: scs@sallystarr.cc
www.sallystarr.cc

Sandscapes, LLC.
1637 Arbor Ridge Dr.
Fort Worth, TX 76112
Tel: 817 937 6077
Email: lauren@sandscapes.net
www.sandscapes.net

TASM Design
19 Lewis Ave.
Winthrop, MA 02152
Tel: 617 733 8510
Email: jennifer@tasmdesign.com
www.tasmdesign.com

West Farm Arts
Newton, MA
Tel: 617 964 1670
Email: ellen@westfarmarts.com
westfarmarts.home.comcast.net

PAINTS AND PRODUCTS
BEHR
Corporate Headquarters
BEHR Process Corporation
3400 West Segerstrom Ave.
Santa Ana, CA 92704
See website for store locator
www.behr.com

California Paints
150 Dascomb Rd.
Andover, MA 01810
Tel: 800 225 1141
See website for store locator
www.californiapaints.com

Devine Color
333 South State St., V-304
Lake Oswego, OR 97034
Tel: 503 675 9519
Tel: 1 866 926 5677
www.devinecolor.com

Devoe Paint
ICI Paints
East Building
15885 West Sprague Rd.
Strongsville, OH 44136
Tel: 440 297 8635
See website for store locator
www.icipaintsinna.com

Farmington Fireplaces
Fireplaces only
Northleach
Cheltenham
Gloucestershire
GL54 3NZ
UK
www.farmington.co.uk
Tel: (UK) 00 44 800 731 0071

Fine Paints of Europe
P.O. Box 419
Rte. 4 West
Woodstock, VT 05091
Tel: 1 800 332 1556
www.fine-paints.com

General Paint
Corporate Office
950 Raymur Ave.
Vancouver, BC V6A 3L5
Tel: 604 253 3131
www.generalpaint.com

Golden Artist Colors, Inc.
188 Bell Rd.
New Berlin, NY 13411-9527
Tel: 607 847 6154
Tel: 1 800 959 6543
www.goldenpaints.com

The Old Fashioned
Milk Paint Co.
436 Main St.
P.O. Box 222
Groton, MA 01450
Tel: 978 448 6336
www.milkpaint.com

Pratt & Lambert, Inc.
P.O. Box 22
Buffalo, NY 14240
Tel: 1 800 Buy Pratt
www.prattandlambert.com

R&F Handmade Paints, Inc.
506 Broadway
Kingston, NY 12401
Tel: 1 800 206 8088
Tel: 845 331 3112
www.rfpaints.com

The Sherwin-Williams Company
101 Prospect Ave. NW
Cleveland, OH 44115
Tel: 1 800 4 SHERWIN
www.sherwin-williams.com

HOME FURNISHINGS
Maine Cottage
P.O. Box 935
Yarmouth, ME 04096
Tel: 1 888 859 5522
www.mainecottage.com

STENCILS AND ARTISTS MATERIALS FOR PAINT EFFECTS
Blue Ribbon Stencils
3451 Wellington Dr.
Dayton, OH 45410
Tel: 937 254 2319
Email: info@blueribbonstencils.com
www.blueribbonstencils.com

Designer Stencils
C/o The Designer Shoppe, Inc.
3634 Silverside Rd.
Wilmington, DE 19810
Tel: 1 800 822 7836
www.designerstencils.com

Dressler Stencil Co.
253 SW 41st St.
Renton, WA 98055-4930
Tel: 888 656 4515
Tel: 425 656 4515
www.dresslerstencils.com

Firenze Enterprises, Inc.
12976 SW 132 Ave.
Miami, FL 33186
Tel: 305 232 0233
www.rivesto-marmorino.com

Henny Donovan Motif
10 Brook Lodge, Coolhurst Rd.
London
N8 8ER
UK
Tel: (UK) 00 44 20 8340 0259
Email: salesinfo@hennydonovan
motif.co.uk
www.hennydonovanmotif.co.uk

Kremer Pigments, Inc.
228 Elizabeth St.
New York, NY 10012
Tel: 212 219 2394
www.kremer-pigmente.de

The Mad Stencilist
P.O. Box 5437
Dept. N
El Dorado Hills, CA 95762
Tel: 1 888 882 6232
www.madstencilist.com

Pearl Paints
308 Canal St.
New York, NY 10013
Tel: 1 800 451 7327
www.pearlpaint.com

Pierre Finkelstein Institute of
Decorative Painting, Inc.
Suite 1009, 20 West 20th St.
New York, NY 10011
Tel: 1 888 FAUX ART
www.pfinkelstein.com

Sepp Leaf Products, Inc.
381 Park Ave. S.
New York, NY 10016
Tel: 212 683 2840
www.seppleaf.com

Sinopia LLC
229 Valencia St.
San Francisco, CA 94103
Tel: 415 621 2898
www.sinopia.com

Stencils by Nancy
19115 Relay Rd.
Humble, TX 77346
Tel: 281 686 1226
www.stencilsbynancy.net

StenSource® International, Inc.
18971 Hess Ave.
Sonora, CA 95370
Tel: 800 642 9293
Email: customerservice@
stensource.com
www.stensource.com

Index

accent colors 10, 12, 104, 126, 127, 180, 184, 232

adjoining rooms 12, 62, 165, 173

aging techniques 193, 194, 195, 198, 200, 202, 203, 219

alcoves 159, 171

alkyd paint *see* latex paint

American Colonial style 34
  bedrooms 150, 151
  hallways 135
  living rooms 180
  palette 141
  sitting rooms 135
  wood staining 206

American neoclassical palette 141

ancient Egyptian palette 209, 215, 223

ancient Grecian style 133, 184
  palette 138
  wall paintings 177

ancient Roman style 209, 215, 217
  palette 134, 138
  sitting rooms 134
  trompe l'oeil 190

antiquing 193, 194, 202, 211, 232

architectural features 17, 49, 65, 95, 114, 133, 134, 215
  highlighting 17, 113, 134, 200, 218
  trompe l'oeil 190

Art Deco style 34, 60
  accessories 133
  bedrooms 150, 151
  palette 144
  patterns 184
  velvet effect 223

Art Nouveau style
  bathrooms 152, 153
  palette 144

Arts and Crafts style
  bedrooms 150
  palette 143
  stencils 188

bamboo 17, 65, 95, 105, 109

Baroque style 134, 177
  faux techniques 219, 221
  palette 140

baseboards 30, 64, 65, 202, 219, 225

base coat 201, 227, 232

bathrooms 13, 226
  exotic colors 91
  faux techniques 209, 210, 211, 215, 217, 220
  historic colors 152, 153
  light-creating colors 169
  Mediterranean colors 83
  natural and neutral colors 18, 19
  paint techniques 187, 188, 191, 203
  pastel colors 34
  space-creating colors 168, 169
  warm and cozy colors 51, 169

Bauhaus palette 133, 145

bedrooms 13
  contemporary colors 112, 113, 118, 128–9
  exotic colors 95, 97, 98, 99, 106–7
  historic colors 134, 137, 150–1
  hot colors 66
  light-creating colors 167, 172, 173
  Mediterranean colors 167
  natural and neutral colors 18, 20, 28–9
  and paint techniques 188, 223
  pastel colors 33, 35
  space-creating colors 156, 166, 167, 172, 173
  warm and cozy colors 48, 49, 53

black 9, 104, 107, 113, 114, 210

blinds 36, 67

blue 81, 82, 101, 102
  spatial aspects 155, 156, 159, 162, 163

bold colors 59, 95, 101, 113, 114, 120
  faux techniques 210, 216, 218, 220
  textural techniques 195, 205

borders 175, 177, 180–1, 196, 216, 217

brass 95, 102

breakfast areas 34, 136

bricks 49, 53

bronzing 13, 211, 216

brown 21, 49, 54, 157, 170, 210, 205

brushes 197, 198, 199, 200, 203, 206, 207, 212, 215, 216, 221, 222, 225, 232

budgeting 228

burgundy 49, 131, 132, 133, 150

cabinets 179, 189, 196, 213

calligraphy 108, 109

Caribbean style 65, 95
  bedrooms 98
  dining rooms 110, 111
  kitchens 98–9
  palette 103

ceilings 11, 12, 52, 65, 85
  paint techniques 180, 181, 215
  sloping ceilings 158–9, 166–7, 168–9
  spatial aspects 155, 156, 163, 164, 165

ceramics 96, 101

children's rooms 178, 226
  bedrooms 12, 13, 65, 178–9
  ceilings 179, 182, 200

Chinese style 95, 106
  accessories 96
  bedrooms 97, 99, 106, 107, 167
  hallways 96
  lacquer technique 213
  living rooms 108, 109
  palette 104

Chinoiserie 97

clouds, paint techniques 179, 182, 200

Colonial style *see* American Colonial style

color
  basics of 7–9
  choosing schemes 11–13, 226–7
  cool colors 9, 17, 81, 155, 156, 162–3
  contrasting colors 9, 10, 11
  harmonizing colors 7, 9, 11
  palettes *see* individual styles
  perception of 8, 155
  spatial aspects 60, 155
  warm colors 9, 49

color washing 13, 49, 195

color wheel 8, 56, 58, 72

combing 196, 209, 220

contemporary style 64, 65, 78–9, 113, 114–19, 126–31
  faux techniques 212, 214, 218, 219, 221, 222
  palette 120–5
  rooms 34, 45, 104, 112, 113, 118, 128–9

corridors 162, 190

costs 177, 228, 231
cottage style *see* rustic style
crackle glaze 197, 232
crackling 193, 197
craquelure 197
curtains *see* drapes and curtains

damasks 49, 50, 95
decoupage 232
dining rooms 4, 226
    contemporary colors 114, 117
    exotic colors 95, 110,111
    faux techniques 209, 214, 218, 223
    historic colors 135, 136
    hot colors 65, 67, 76–7
    light-creating colors 171
    Mediterranean colors 83, 84–5
    pastel colors 34
    space-creating colors 170, 171
    textural techniques 177, 183, 199
    warm and cozy colors 49, 51, 170
distressing 193, 198, 232
do-it-yourself 13, 228–30
    see also individual paint techniques
doors 17, 30, 31, 226
    paint techniques 196, 199, 204, 205,
        219, 225
dragging 193, 199
drapes and curtains 11, 76, 77, 95, 113,
    128, 135, 172, 185
dry brushing 200

Edwardian style 153
eggshell-finish paint 215, 223, 225,
    226, 227
eighties style 133
    bedrooms 134
    palette 149
entryways *see* hallways and entranceways
equipment 229–30
exotic style
    palettes 100–5
    rooms 94, 96–9, 106–11

faux techniques 13, 175, 191, 208–25
feature walls 11
    contemporary colors 128, 129, 130,
        131

natural and neutral colors 28–9
paint techniques 215, 210, 222
warm and cozy colors 61, 75, 155,
    173
fifties style 78, 136
    palette 146
fireplaces 11, 171, 183
    contemporary colors 115, 126,
        127
    exotic colors 97
    historic colors 136
    hot colors 66
    Mediterranean colors 84
    natural and neutral colors 16, 17
    paint techniques 212, 215
    pastel colors 35
    warm and cozy colors 49, 60–1, 157
fixtures and fittings 96, 99, 228
floors 10, 12, 91
    contemporary colors 115, 131,
        135
    exotic colors 98–9
    hot colors 64, 65, 75, 77, 78–9
    Mediterranean colors 82, 92, 93
    natural and neutral colors 17, 18, 20,
        30, 31
    paint techniques 177, 181, 184, 188,
        203, 215, 217, 225
    pastel colors 36, 44, 45
    spatial aspects 154, 155, 156, 158,
        163, 164, 165
    warm and cozy colors 61
floral patterns 33, 133, 150, 184,
    185, 193
    borders 181
    handpainting 179
    stencils 177, 188, 189
flowers 16, 52, 82, 114
    see also floral patterns
focal points 12, 17, 46, 53, 60, 93, 108,
    109, 155, 222
forties style 202
    bedrooms 150
    palette 145
fratting *see* frottage
fresco 13, 177, 182–3, 193
frieze 180, 181, 232
frottage 201

furniture 11, 12
    paint techniques 183, 186, 193, 194,
        196, 197, 198, 199, 200, 202, 203,
        204, 205

Georgian style 17, 21, 138
    bathrooms 153
    bedrooms 150, 151
    dining rooms 135, 136
    palette 140
    velvet effect 223
gilding 211, 232
glass 11, 33, 65, 113
glazes 199, 201, 202, 215, 216, 221,
    225, 232
gold 65, 102, 104, 134, 194, 209
    and paint techniques 194, 209, 210,
        211, 216
    walls 52, 94, 95, 97, 106, 107
Gothic style
    faux techniques 214, 216, 221, 223
    hallways 133
    palette 139
    see also Medieval style
graining 196, 225
granite effect 212
gray 17, 116, 117, 118, 119, 120, 126,
    180–1, 216
Greece 81, 91
green 102, 138, 150, 165

hallways and entranceways 226
    light-creating colors 164, 165
    Mediterranean colors 82, 84
    natural and neutral colors 30–1
    paint techniques 190, 208, 209
    space-creating colors 154, 155, 158,
        164
    warm and cozy colors 62–3, 159, 165
handpainting 178, 179, 189
hot housing style
    palette 68–73
    rooms 65, 66–7, 74–9
hues 7–8

Indian style 11, 65, 67, 68
    accessories 95, 96
    bedrooms 107

Indian style *continued*
  borders 180
  dining rooms 110, 111
  living rooms 97
  palette 102
interior designers 230–1, 233–4
Islamic style 94, 95, 97, 99
  bathrooms 91
  bedrooms 106
  dining rooms 110, 111
  palette 101
  see also Moroccan style
Italy 81, 137, 215

Japanese style
  accessories 95
  bedrooms 106
  dining rooms 111
  living rooms 109
  palette 105

kitchens 6, 7, 10, 11, 226
  cabinets 78, 79, 82, 199,
    219
  contemporary colors 114, 115, 119
    130–1
  exotic colors 98–9
  historic colors 136
  hot colors 65, 66, 67, 78–9
  light-creating colors 158
  Mediterranean colors 82, 130
  paint techniques 183, 195, 203, 207,
    212, 213, 217
  pastel colors 33, 34
  space-creating colors 157, 158–9
  warm and cozy colors 49

lacquer 104, 213, 232
latex paint 226, 227
laundry rooms 226
leather effect 213, 214
leopard-skin effect 50, 210
libraries 49, 214
light 8, 9, 12, 60, 62, 65, 129, 155,
    156, 162–3
  light-creating colors 161
lighting 51, 52, 154, 155, 159
lime 94, 95
liming 203, 232
living rooms 12
  contemporary colors 114, 116, 117,
    118, 119, 126–7

exotic colors 11, 95, 96, 97, 98, 108,
    109
historic colors 133, 134, 135, 137
hot colors 64, 74–5
Mediterranean colors 82, 84, 85, 90–1,
    92–3
natural and neutral colors 19, 20, 21
paint techniques 183, 191, 199, 210,
    214, 217, 222, 223
pastel colors 32, 33, 35, 36, 37, 44–5,
    46–7
space-creating colors 156
warm and cozy colors 49, 50, 51, 52,
    53, 61, 118, 156, 163
loft rooms 112, 113

marble 96, 97, 191
marbling techniques 13, 202, 209, 215
materials 226–8, 235
Matisse, Henri 184
matte-finish paint 65, 113, 120, 130, 232
Medieval style 189
  bathrooms 152
  faux techniques 219, 221, 223
  kitchens 189
  palette 139
  see also Gothic style
Mediterranean style
  and faux techniques 217, 218
  palette 86–9
  rooms 12, 51, 80, 81, 82–5, 90–3, 130
metallic effects 216
metalwork 96, 97, 101, 113, 175, 198,
    209
  painting 227
Mexican style
  bedrooms 107
  borders 180
  dining rooms 95, 110
  palette 100
Middle Eastern style *see* Islamic style
minimalist style 12, 133, 195
modern style *see* contemporary style
moldings 113, 158, 180, 190, 200, 202,
    218, 219
monochromatic color schemes 7, 92, 128
Moroccan style
  accessories 97
  bedrooms 107, 167
  dining rooms 111
  living rooms 95, 96, 97
  see also Islamic style

Morris, William 150, 188, 224
mosaic effect 209, 217
murals 175, 182

natural materials 65, 81
naturals and neutrals
  and contemporary colors 113, 120, 122,
    126, 127, 129, 131
  and exotic colors 95, 108–9
  faux techniques 209
  palette 22–7
  rooms 17, 18–21, 28–31, 162, 163
  and warm and cozy colors 61
neoclassical style 52, 61, 136, 137, 141
  paint techniques 182, 183, 203, 207
nineties style 133
  palette 149
nurseries *see* children's rooms

offices *see* studies
oil-based paint 226, 227
open-plan design 118
orange 49, 81, 103, 180–1

paint
  durability 49, 126, 226, 227
  equipment 229
  pigment-based 138
  suppliers 234–5
  swatches 12
  techniques 174–225
  tips for using 229
  types 226, 227
paint and wallpaper contractors 230–1
palettes *see* color
paneling 82, 158, 168, 186, 198, 203,
    206, 207, 214
  faux techniques 208, 209, 216, 220,
    222, 224, 225
pastel style
  palette 38–43
  rooms 9, 11, 33, 34–7, 44–7, 133,
    151
patterns 11, 33, 49, 74, 133, 150, 175,
    177
  abstract 197
  check 177, 185
  dot 185, 186, 207
  geometric prints 33, 113, 133, 177,
    180–1, 184
  paint techniques 180, 184–5, 187,
    196, 202, 206

stripes 18, 19, 20, 33, 35, 77
repeating 184, 188, 204
see also floral patterns
period style see individual periods
picture rails 180, 226, 232
pictures, painted 175–91
plaster 194, 197, 198, 218
plaster effect 218
powder rooms 186, 190
preparation of surfaces 209, 228
primary colors 8
primer 227, 232
professionals, hiring 13, 178, 182, 193, 209, 230–1
project management 231
purple 95, 97, 99, 101, 138, 156

ragging 13, 175, 202, 204, 209, 232
rainbows 7–8, 95, 178
recessed walls 60–1
see also feature walls
red 52, 68, 101, 102, 107, 155
Regency style
bedrooms 97
stencils 188
Rococo style
bedrooms 137, 151
palette 137, 142
rustic style 12, 35, 52, 81, 85, 198, 206, 218, 222
rusting 13, 219

scenes, painted 177, 182
scumble see glazes
secondary colors 8
seventies style 133
bathrooms 152, 153
faux techniques 224
palette 148
shading techniques 195, 201
Shaker style 134
bathrooms 153
bedrooms 95
palette 142
shutters 46, 80, 81
sideboards 186, 206
silk effect 220
silver 65, 66, 102, 127, 211, 216
sisal 17, 103

sixties style 74–5
bedrooms 150, 151
palette 147
small rooms 156, 157, 160, 166–7
Southeast Asian style 98
speckling 212, 229
sponging 13, 17, 81, 133, 175, 179, 205, 211, 212, 232
staining 196, 206, 226, 232
stairways 30–1, 62–3, 84, 114, 117, 183, 188, 226
light-creating colors 164, 165
Mediterranean colors 165
space-creating colors 164
stamping 179, 188–9, 199
stenciling 13, 177, 178, 179, 180, 181, 188, 189, 216, 224, 235
stippling 13, 17, 49, 193, 207, 212, 221
stone 24, 26, 66, 134, 175
block effect 209, 221
finishes 180, 190, 191, 197, 204, 215
textures 49, 65, 103, 105
striped patterns 18, 19, 20, 33, 35, 77, 162, 163, 177, 184, 186, 187
borders 180–1
children's rooms 179
combing 196
studies 18, 36, 162–163
suede effect 222

terra-cotta 62, 81, 82, 100, 194
tertiary colors 8
textures 11, 12, 49, 103, 120
paint techniques 17, 81, 103, 133
soft furnishings 95, 65, 113
thirties style 199, 202, 207
tiles 62, 80, 81, 83, 101, 115, 186, 187, 202, 217
tints 9, 11
tonal values 10–11, 12, 29, 30, 31, 51, 52, 101
tracing 179, 180
trompe l'oeil 13, 133, 177, 190, 191, 221
tropical style see exotic style
Tudor style 214, 219

undercoat see base coat
urban style 219

varnish 188, 197, 219, 226, 232
velvet effect 223

verandas 84–5
Victorian style 48, 49, 54, 132, 133, 224
bathrooms 152
bedrooms 150, 151
dining rooms 171
and paint techniques 188, 202, 223
palette 143
see also Arts and Crafts style

wallpaper 177, 180, 182, 202, 224, 227–8, 230
wallpaper paint effect 224
Warhol, Andy 74, 75
warm and cozy palette 54–9
and contemporary colors 112, 113, 114, 117
and exotic colors 108
and historic colors 136
and hot colors 65, 66, 75, 76, 77, 78, 79
and Mediterranean colors 81, 84, 85, 90, 91, 93
and pastel colors 9, 33, 44, 45, 46, 47
rooms 49, 50–3, 60–3, 81
warmth-creating palette 161
white 9, 17, 33, 40, 113, 152
wicker 17, 18, 40, 48, 49
window areas 46–7, 128–9, 152–3, 156, 168, 191
wood 11, 65, 66, 76, 80, 81, 175, 226
contemporary colors 114, 115, 117
exotic colors 95, 97, 104, 106
historic colors 135   40, 117
hot colors 65, 66, 76
Mediterranean colors 80, 81, 82, 83, 90, 91
natural and neutral colors 17, 19, 21, 30
paint techniques 194, 195, 196, 197, 198, 203, 225
pastel colors 33, 34, 36, 40, 44, 45, 46
staining 206
warm and cozy colors 48, 49, 50, 63
wooden floorboards 30, 31, 45, 135, 187
wrought-iron furniture 81

yellow 81, 82, 180
yin and yang 104, 107

zebra-skin effect 210

Acknowledgments

The publishers would like to thank the following companies for their assistance: Anna Rodé Designs, Inc., Bauer Interior Design, California Paints, Devoe Paint, Dressler Stencil Co. Inc., Farmington Fireplaces, Integral Color Design for Architecture and Interiors, Maine Cottage, The Rohm & Haas Paint Quality Institute, Sandscapes LLC, The Sherwin Williams Company.

Cover: front left Elizabeth Whiting & Associates, front center and right Redcover, back left Maine Cottage/Dennis Welsh, back right Elizabeth Whiting & Associates
1 Maine Cottage/Dennis Welsh
2 Farmington Fireplaces
6 Elizabeth Whiting & Associates
7 Maine Cottage/Dennis Welsh
10–11 Bauer Interior Design
12 Elizabeth Whiting & Associates
13b The Sherwin Williams Company
13t & 14 Elizabeth Whiting & Associates
16 Farmington Fireplaces
18br Elizabeth Whiting & Associates
18l & 18tr Maine Cottage/Dennis Welsh
19bl Bauer Interior Design
19br Maine Cottage/Dennis Welsh
19tl Coleen Choisser/Anna Rodé Designs, Inc.
20bl & 20c Elizabeth Whiting & Associates
20tl Maine Cottage/Dennis Welsh
21br Farmington Fireplaces
21tr California Paints
28–30 Elizabeth Whiting & Associates
32 & 34br Maine Cottage/Dennis Welsh
34l Elizabeth Whiting & Associates
34tr California Paints
35bl & 35br Maine Cottage/Dennis Welsh
35t Farmington Fireplaces
36r Maine Cottage/Dennis Welsh
36tl Elizabeth Whiting & Associates
37b Devoe Paint
37bl Elizabeth Whiting & Associates
37t & 44–46 Maine Cottage/Dennis Welsh
48 Elizabeth Whiting & Associates
50bl Coleen Choisser/Anna Rodé Designs, Inc.
50r Elizabeth Whiting & Associates
50tl Devoe Paint
51l Coleen Choisser/Anna Rodé Designs, Inc.
51r & 52 Elizabeth Whiting & Associates
53b Maine Cottage/Dennis Welsh
53t California Paints
60 Farmington Fireplaces
62–64 & 66br Elizabeth Whiting & Associates
66l Farmington Fireplaces
66tr, 67–80 & 82bl Elizabeth Whiting & Associates
82r Coleen Choisser/Anna Rodé Designs, Inc.
82tl Maine Cottage/Dennis Welsh
83b The Rohm & Haas Paint Quality Institute
83t & 84bl Coleen Choisser/Anna Rodé Designs, Inc.
84c Maine Cottage/Dennis Welsh
84tl Devoe Paint
85–96 Elizabeth Whiting & Associates
97bl The Rohm & Haas Paint Quality Institute
97br Marv Sloben/Anna Rodé Designs, Inc.
97tl & 97tr Elizabeth Whiting & Associates
98bl The Rohm & Haas Paint Quality Institute
98c Elizabeth Whiting & Associates
98tl The Rohm & Haas Paint Quality Institute
99br Elizabeth Whiting & Associates
99tr Maine Cottage/Dennis Welsh

106–108 Elizabeth Whiting & Associates
110 The Sherwin Williams Company
112 Abode Interiors Picture Library
114bl Coleen Choisser/Anna Rodé Designs, Inc.
114br Maine Cottage/Dennis Welsh
114tr & 115bl Elizabeth Whiting & Associates
115tl Bauer Interior Design
115tr Farmington Fireplaces
116bl Maine Cottage/Dennis Welsh
116c Elizabeth Whiting & Associates
116tl & 117br Devoe Paint
117tr Abode Interiors Picture Library
118bl & 118r Devoe Paint
118tl & 119b Coleen Choisser/Anna Rodé Designs, Inc.
119t Devoe Paint
126–128 Elizabeth Whiting & Associates
130 Bauer Interior Design
132 Elizabeth Whiting & Associates
134bl Bauer Interior Design
134br Marv Sloben/Anna Rodé Designs, Inc.
134tr California Paints
135bl Maine Cottage/Dennis Welsh
135br The Rohm & Haas Paint Quality Institute
135t Elizabeth Whiting & Associates
136bl Maine Cottage/Dennis Welsh
136r Bauer Interior Design
136tl California Paints
137–150 The Rohm & Haas Paint Quality Institute
152 Bauer Interior Design
154, 156br & 156l Elizabeth Whiting & Associates
156tr Abode Interiors Picture Library
157b Farmington Fireplaces
157t & 158bl The Rohm & Haas Paint Quality Institute
158c & 158tl Elizabeth Whiting & Associates
159br The Rohm & Haas Paint Quality Institute
159tr Elizabeth Whiting & Associates
162 Sandscapes LLC/Lauren Childs
164 The Rohm & Haas Paint Quality Institute
166–176, 178bl Elizabeth Whiting & Associates
178r Jan Dressler/Dressler Stencil Co. Inc.
178tl Tim France
179 Elizabeth Whiting & Associates
180 Bauer Interior Design
181br Jan Dressler/Dressler Stencil Co. Inc.
181cr & 181tl Elizabeth Whiting & Associates
181tr Barbara Jacobs/Integral Color Design for Architecture and Interiors
183bl & 183br Elizabeth Whiting & Associates
183cl Coleen Choisser/Anna Rodé Designs, Inc.

183tl Barbara Jacobs/Integral Color Design for Architecture and Interiors
183tr Elizabeth Whiting & Associates
184l Bauer Interior Design
184r & 185bl Elizabeth Whiting & Associates
185br & 185tl Paul Forrester
185tr Sandscapes LLC/Lauren Childs
186bl Tim France
186br Elizabeth Whiting & Associates
186tl Barbara Jacobs/Integral Color Design for Architecture and Interiors
186tr Bauer Interior Design
187l Barbara Jacobs/Integral Color Design for Architecture and Interiors
187r Paul Forrester
188bl Barbara Jacobs/Integral Color Design for Architecture and Interiors
188br Tim Ridley
188l Paul Forrester
188tl Paul Forrester, Colin Bowling
188tr John Freeman
189 Tim Ridley
182 Coleen Choisser/Anna Rodé Designs, Inc.
190 & 191b Jan Dressler/Dressler Stencil Co. Inc.
191t Paul Forrester
192 Elizabeth Whiting & Associates
194 Sandscapes LLC/Lauren Childs
195–197 The Sherwin Williams Company
198 Tim France
199 Elizabeth Whiting & Associates
200 Paul Forrester, Colin Bowling
201 Tim France
202 Barbara Jacobs/Integral Color Design for Architecture and Interiors
203–204 Tim Ridley
205 The Sherwin Williams Company
206 Elizabeth Whiting & Associates
207 Paul Forrester
208 Paul Forrester, Colin Bowling
210 Elizabeth Whiting & Associates
211b The Sherwin Williams Company
211t Coleen Choisser/Anna Rodé Designs, Inc.
212b Barbara Jacobs/Integral Color Design for Architecture and Interiors
212t Sandscapes LLC/Lauren Childs
213 Elizabeth Whiting & Associates
214 Sandscapes LLC/Lauren Childs
215bl Coleen Choisser/Anna Rodé Designs, Inc.
215br Tim Ridley
215t Barbara Jacobs/Integral Color Design for Architecture and Interiors
216–217 Paul Forrester, Colin Bowling
218 Bauer Interior Design
219 Tim France
220 Barbara Jacobs/Integral Color Design for Architecture and Interiors
221–222 Sandscapes LLC/Lauren Childs
223 The Sherwin Williams Company
224 Paul Forrester, Colin Bowling
225 Tim Ridley